Advance Praise for *Expecting Money*

"I recognize practical, effective and down-to-earth advice when I read it. However, *Expecting Money* goes far beyond that and is wonderful! . . . A must-read for new parents."

—**GLINDA BRIDGFORTH,** founder of Bridgforth Financial and author of *Girl, Get Your Credit Straight!*

"*Expecting Money* dispels the myth that one has to be rich to attain financial security. Erica's personal experiences with her own family along with her professional expertise . . . make *Expecting Money* a practical, insightful must-read for all couples and parents."

—**BETTY T. YEE,** Chairwoman, California State Board of Equalization

"I highly recommend *Expecting Money*. Use it to take an enormous step closer to creating a practical financial plan that works for you and your family."

—**ROMANUS WOLTER,** The Kick Start Guy, Author, Speaker, *Entrepreneur* magazine's Success Coach

"In *Ex*   arents-
to-be   their
finan   baby."

"Eric   nt to
read a   le she
covers   —and
   d   "

Expecting
MONEY

Expecting
MONEY

*The Essential Financial Plan
for New and Growing Families*

ERICA SANDBERG

KAPLAN PUBLISHING

New York

Vice President and Publisher: Maureen McMahon
Editorial Director: Jennifer Farthing
Acquisitions Editor: Shannon Berning
Development Editor: Eric Titner
Production Editor: Julio Espin
Book Designer: Ivelisse Robles Marrero
Typesetter: Todd Bowman
Cover Designer: Rod Hernandez

© 2008 by Erica Sandberg

Published by Kaplan Publishing, a division of Kaplan, Inc.
1 Liberty Plaza, 24th Floor
New York, NY 10006

Printed in the United States of America

January 2008
10 9 8 7 6 5 4 3 2 1

ISBN-13: 978-1-4277-9594-6

Table of Contents

Introduction

WHEN I BECAME PREGNANT with my daughter Lillian, I was caught off guard by how little I—someone who has been in the personal finance field for over a decade—knew about the monetary aspects of pregnancy and new parenthood. I am a planner by nature and wanted to know everything: what I should and shouldn't buy, how taking time off to care for my newborn would impact my income, what budgetary decisions my husband and I needed to make together, and so much more. Every question led to another. It seemed that each person I polled, from my mother, friends, and sisters to total strangers, had a different response. I turned to books, magazines, and websites, and again, they offered either contradictory or incomplete advice. I craved clear, well-researched information, all in one place. Frankly, I wanted a book just like *Expecting Money*—which didn't yet exist.

Ultimately, my reasons for writing this book were both personal and professional. For the past decade, I have been with Consumer Credit

Counseling Service of San Francisco, a nonprofit organization that helps people from all walks of life overcome financial problems. During that time, I have done everything from individual client counseling to facilitating large-scale workshops and seminars and acting as primary media advisor for local and national news outlets. Each year, I have witnessed and advised on the same struggles: so many people were consistently making choices that harmed rather than helped their circumstances. I wanted to help put an end to this disturbing trend of plummeting personal savings and escalating consumer debt. As a nation, we are indeed in trouble. As individuals, we can absolutely turn the tide toward healthy financial decision making.

I've also had the opportunity to speak with countless pregnant women and new mothers and fathers about the economic impact of parenthood. The majority expressed similar experiences and frustrations. They told me about the money they spent on all the baby items they didn't need or use, about not really knowing if quitting their job was the right decision, about being blindsided by childcare and medical expenses. I heard from those who were trying to conceive or adopt express their fears and concerns about the high costs involved in doing so; single parents lamented the difficulties of being a sole provider; and two-parent families shared the conflicts caused by so many extra expenditures. Across the board, I found that being unprepared led to waste and, often, debt. This is a tragedy, because today's new parents can ill afford to throw away one single dime. Life is just too expensive.

My intention in writing *Expecting Money* was to help every new parent develop a practical and enlightening financial plan. By providing accurate, objective information about the most common and pressing concerns, it's my goal to motivate you to analyze your world, explore and refine your financial values, and to take well-informed actions that will ensure a brighter future for yourself and your children.

This book begins and ends with detailed financial assessments of the foremost economic issues that affect most new parents. There are many worksheets to complete and quizzes to take—each designed to guide you toward a better understanding of yourself and what needs to be done to improve your finances and attain your goals. To help you prepare for all the pre- and postpartum costs, I made every effort to have as few vague "well, it depends" responses as possible regarding how much one could expect to pay for these key expenses. In the end, providing specifics was a considerable challenge. The fact is, the United States is a massive country, and regional variances are significant. An item or service that costs $25 in Grand Forks, North Dakota, may be three times that in New York City. Therefore, many times I give price ranges, which will provide you with an effective starting point to begin planning.

In the middle of writing this book, my grandmother passed away. I don't think she knew what an inspiration she was to me, especially when it came to finances. She was shrewd and sharp; she not only lived through the Great Depression, she thrived from it. A self-taught investor, she "played the market" and, as a relatively young widow, supported herself in style with the money she made through remarkably astute trades. Her unwavering belief that it is always possible to set some cash aside, even during the worst of times, was compelling. Economic independence was her driving force. On the day she died, she held my hand and said, "Save your money, Erica." I told her not to worry.

As parents, it is our responsibility to create a safe and secure financial platform for our children. The pressures to overspend and undersave are intense, but we've got to overcome them. If *Expecting Money* does anything, I hope it shows you that you have the power to defy debt, spend your hard-earned money on things that you truly love, and make your dreams a reality through saving and investing.

Treat your money with respect and handle it wisely. Your growing family is worth the effort.

Chapter 1

Getting Started

Where Are You Now?

A S YOU ARE UNDOUBTEDLY aware, this is a unique and special time in your life. Whether you are pregnant now or have recently had your baby, this is an ideal opportunity for you to reflect, learn, decide, prepare, and act, all for the greater financial good of your growing family. Therefore, making the most of this time is crucial. Rather than just being accountable for yourself, you are now (or soon will be) responsible for the well-being of a completely new life, one whom you'll love and who is completely dependent upon you for her care.

Sound serious? It is, but in a wonderful way. Becoming a parent is often a lightbulb-popping "wow, I need to get it together" moment in which people make profound life changes. So if your heart is starting to beat a bit faster just thinking about the state of your finances and what the future holds, *that's okay.* You'll soon be putting that nervous energy to good use. *Expecting Money* will not only show you how to confront any money obstacle you may be facing as you plan your family's future, it will also teach you to identify and use your resources to your advantage. However intimidating it may seem right now, preparing for your family's financial well-being is a winnable challenge, one worth your best effort. Soon you'll have all the tools and strategies necessary to help get you ready for the economic side of parenthood.

If you're expecting, it's a good idea to tie up as many financial loose ends as possible now, so you can focus on all of the other wonderful baby moments that await you. While the outside world may seem less important, your gas and electric company, strangely enough, will still want to get paid, and you'll need to summon the energy to do so.

The moment your baby appears on the scene, he, not the state of your financial affairs, is going to be your primary concern, and you may find that making rational decisions isn't as easy as it was before. When you're holding that tiny being in your arms for the first time, lavishing her with the best money can buy may very well feel like the right thing to do. Nevertheless, that bill will soon be in your mailbox. It's in your best interest to develop sound financial habits. The more efficiently you deal with money matters now, the more time you'll have to focus on other parenting issues later.

As you go through this book, keep in mind the following statement: *the financial security of your family is paramount.* While that declaration may sound dramatic and obvious, it can be easy to forget, especially considering that your life is about to change drastically. Besides, there'll be a lot of other, more pleasant things to think about during parenthood. Money problems make life more difficult, and the consequences of ignoring your finances can be disastrous. Isn't this the *last thing* you want to happen as you welcome a new life into your family?

It's important to realize that family finances are more than just opening a college savings plan. Nike only had it part right with its famous tagline "Just do it." Taking action is key, but to make sound decisions, you'll also need to have solid, comprehensive information in your corner. Furthermore, you've got to be organized and motivated. This book will teach you the following:

- To prioritize your spending by defining and refining your money values

- To manage debt and use credit to your advantage
- All about the costs of having a baby and how to plan for the broad spectrum of health care expenses that arise as your family grows
- Where to splurge and when to save, so you can get what you really need and enjoy what you wont
- How to communicate with your partner about money—techniques that can bring you closer and reduce the tension that financial problems often bring about
- How single parents can raise a family on one income and how and why to pursue child support
- The best ways to make work "work" for you, from stay-at-home parenting to income alternatives
- How to gain the most from your employee benefits package
- What the various caregiver options are and which works best for you
- How to set and achieve all of your family's financial goals—whether it's a new home, fabulous vacation, or anything in-between
- How to budget for what you need today and plan for what you'll want tomorrow

USE YOUR EMOTIONS TO YOUR ADVANTAGE

When it comes to money, most new and expecting parents generally have two emotions regarding money: fear and desire. They often have lofty dreams and goals for their family but are afraid of making a decision (or *not* making a decision) that could jeopardize their security. Fortunately, you can make these emotions work *for* you. Use them to motivate you to practice good spending and saving behaviors and propel you toward achieving your family's financial goals.

Dealing with financial issues can be challenging for many expectant parents, and for good reason. The baby product market is out of control, with the sheer number of "must-have" items getting larger and more expensive every day. Just a few years ago, for example, new parents never gave a thought to buying a "wipe warmer"—they didn't even exist!

Why would we need a special diaper disposable system? Our parents used the trash can. Just thinking about all the costly things that advertisers, friends, and family tell you that you can't live without can frazzle your nerves.

If you're struggling to make ends meet now, you may be wondering how in the world you're going to add the cost of raising a child into the mix without descending into or deeper into debt. This can be a mighty scary prospect. However, don't give up! Use the strategies and advice in this book to transform and improve your situation.

Yet another common fear is that of not having enough money to give your child the life you want for him or her. If you don't like the way you're living now, you probably don't want your child to grow up under those circumstances either. Living on the financial edge is unpleasant enough when you're an adult, but the arrival of a baby can make the situation even more discouraging. It is a horrible feeling to not be able to provide adequately for your child. It's important to remember that planning early and making wise, well-considered decisions now is critical to achieving that objective.

While fear is a common reaction when facing money issues, you shouldn't fear *fear.* This feeling is completely normal, and as long as you don't let it consume and paralyze you, fear can be the ideal motivator to get you to where you need and want to go. I have seen people make some of the most incredible life transformations when they realize their baby's well-being is at stake.

Desire is another powerful feeling that you can make work for you. The craving to give everything to your child is natural. It can inspire you to make more money, go back to school, begin a savings account, purchase the right insurance, or buy a home. Without desire, you don't have dreams.

Unfortunately, a few emotional factors may work against you if you aren't careful. First, making real and lasting financial change is a challenge and often entails breaking former bad habits and implementing new, healthier ones. Change *can* be difficult work, especially over an extended period, but it can be done. Keep your goals in mind and embrace change! Your life is going to change anyway, so seize the reins, and do whatever you can to move things in the best possible direction. Make a pledge to improve upon the way you view and treat money.

At the end of this book, you will be constructing a new and improved family budget with it. You'll be able to distribute your money in ways that make the most sense for you. Although this may mean giving up some immediate pleasures for the greater financial good, know that won't be as hard as it sounds—and remember you're not alone. Almost all of us have to forgo something today to achieve what we want tomorrow. If you've ever tried to quit something that you enjoy, whether your vice was cigarettes, donuts, or indulgences far more harmful to your body and spirit, then you're already aware of how it feels to resist. However, the potential rewards—lasting health and happiness to name a few—make it a worthwhile trade-off.

The desire to focus on all of the fun things that await you once your baby arrives can also be an obstacle. Just remember, responsible decisions must be made. Think about how much attention and energy you've already devoted to naming your child, picking out the colors for his nursery, or choosing a crib and compare that to the time you've spent ensuring that your child will be living in a financially secure environment. Which is more important to your family's current and future lifestyle? You know the answer. This is not to say that budgeting concerns must *always* take center stage, but their importance should never be forgotten or ignored.

OVERCOMING FINANCIAL INERTIA

Think for a moment: when was the last time you analyzed your financial situation in detail? Developed a budget? Planned for the future? If you're like most Americans, it was a long time ago, if ever, and you may not have done it thoroughly enough for it to have been enlightening or effective in any lasting sense. Regardless of what you've done in the past, with a new baby here or on the way, what you do now is what matters most, and getting started is an important step.

Overcoming *financial inertia,* the inability to shift in any direction, much less the right one, can be a real challenge. No matter how much you recognize the importance of facing your personal money issues head-on, you may be tempted to choose avoidance over confrontation. Where does all this resistance stem from? Typically, avoidance comes from feeling overwhelmed by the massive tasks that await you, whether perceived or real. It also comes from not wanting to face the unpleasant business of coming to terms with past mistakes. Eventually, you're going to have to deal with your past financial decisions, whether you want to or not. Take the opportunity to learn from your mistakes and embrace your successes as you move forward towards creating the future you want your family to have.

It is time to stop procrastinating and start doing, and there's every reason to begin immediately. Not only is getting all this money business together fun (I promise!), but the ultimate motivator has landed directly in your lap: your new baby. No other more powerful force for positive change exists.

More than purchasing adorable musical mobiles or colorful booties, you need to protect your child with the gift of security.

FINANCIAL SECURITY: IT'S NOT JUST WHAT YOU THINK

True financial security is not and never will be defined as "high income." Many people make six figure salaries yet are in economic peril because their spending still exceeds their earnings. It has absolutely nothing to do with buying luxury items, living in a grand home, or taking exotic vacations.

So what is it? Financial security is having real control over your money and being prepared for the future. Wouldn't you love to be able to overcome any economic hurdle, whether a sudden job loss, an unforeseen health problem, or an unexpected major expense, without shedding a tear or experiencing financial panic? Trust me, with the proper planning, you can.

Currently, the average U.S. citizen saves less than 1 percent of her net income. The typical credit card holder owes many thousands of dollars in unsecured loans. In fact, for the first time ever, Americans owe more money than they make. According to a May 2006 study by the Center for American Progress, household debt levels have surpassed household income by more than 8 percent, reaching 108.4 percent in 2005. In addition, the Federal Reserve Board reports consumer debt is now at a record $2.17 trillion. If you feel like you're just barely holding it together, take note—you are hardly alone.

Again, I must emphasize that I am not advocating putting money above the love of your baby. However, dealing with financial concerns early on in your child's life is wise. According to the U.S. Department of Agriculture's 2003 report on family expenditures, the cost involved in raising a baby to age 18 is between $130,000 and $261,000, a considerable sum for most people. I am also not implying that your primary aim should be to achieve great wealth. Money alone will not make your family a happy one. Greed is an ugly thing, and the love of money can certainly be a negative and destructive force. Nevertheless, money is important, and you should do whatever you can to make sure that the financial security of your family is in the best possible shape.

Achieving financial security means taking responsibility for planned future costs, preparing for any inevitable crises, and always being in charge of how your money is spent, saved, and invested. The feeling this type of stability provides is amazing, and once you have it, you will never let it go. Even if you're not there yet, the process of spending within your means while saving for the future can make you feel incredibly powerful. Instead of being controlled by your finances, *you* dictate where your money goes.

So what happens when you are financially *insecure*? For starters, it can be a dreadful feeling. Debt and other money woes are leading causes of depression, anxiety, poor work performance (which can lead to unemployment, thus dramatically worsening the problem), and discord within a partner relationship.

Are you financially secure? Take the following quiz and find out. Read each statement carefully and decide if it describes your family's current financial situation. Answer yes or no for each.

QUIZ: Are You Financially Secure?

1. My credit card balances are at zero.
2. I know how much my monthly essential livings expenses are.
3. I have cash reserves in a savings account that equal at least three months of my essential living expenses.
4. If I lost my job, I would be able to find another that pays a similar income in a few months.

5. I feel good when I think about my finances.
6. If I had to fly across country, I would be able to purchase the tickets without having to put the cost on my credit card.
7. I can easily live on 60 percent of my current income for the next couple of months.
8. I regularly check my credit report and know my credit score.
9. My health insurance coverage is enough so that if I had a major medical problem, hospital bills wouldn't force me into bankruptcy.
10. I know the balances of all of my accounts: checking, savings, money market, IRAs, and so on.
11. If the money I have in my current investment vehicles devalues dramatically, I'll be okay.
12. If I am unable to pay for what is owed on my home, vehicle, or other secured loan, I know exactly what to do to prevent its loss.
13. I know the amount of money I spend for all of my expenses on a monthly basis.
14. I consistently save for the future.
15. I enjoy my money without having to go into debt to purchase the things I desire.

The more "yes" responses you make, the more financially secure you likely are. The fewer you make, the more work you'll need to do:

- 12–15 positive responses = Excellent. You are financially secure at this time. Now create an even better future!
- 8–11 positive responses = Good. You are well on the path towards financial security. It won't take much to reach today's and tomorrow's goals.
- 4–10 positive responses = Satisfactory. While there is work to be done, you have set up some great financial safety nets. Build on your successes.
- 0–3 positive responses = Needs work. You have a way to go to achieve financial security, but change starts with self-awareness. Don't despair—take action!

NERVOUS ABOUT YOUR FINANCIAL FUTURE? YOU'RE NOT ALONE!

Interestingly, the fact that desiring and achieving financial security is of vital importance to most pregnant women and new parents has been all but ignored by the media, financial planners, and even many experts in the baby and parenting business. However, I am keenly aware of its significance, not only because I've advised countless expecting parents and families over the decade but also because I was once one of those women.

Although I had worked in the personal finance field for many years, when I became pregnant, I realized just how little I knew about what would happen to my finances after my daughter was born. I didn't know how my budget would change, what child care costs would be, or the amount I would need to spend on baby products. This left me extremely frustrated and very nervous. How on earth was I expected to plan when I didn't know what the future held?

I was hardly alone. Money issues are among the most prominent fears that pregnant women have. In a June 2005 online survey conducted by GCI Group and Equation Research, designed to evaluate the greatest concerns of expectant and new mothers, the following issues came out on top:

- Money (56 percent)
- Losing pregnancy weight (47 percent)
- Baby's health (44 percent)
- Lack of sleep (27 percent)
- Balancing work and child rearing (26 percent)
- Parenting skills (20 percent)
- Breast-feeding (20 percent)

* Source: GCI Group and Equation Research June 2005 online survey, commissioned by Whole Foods Market to evaluate the attitudes of expectant and new moms toward health, natural and organic products, and their babies. The sample consisted of expectant moms currently pregnant or new moms with children not older than six months randomly selected from a licensed research-only panel in the continental United States. A total of 2,344 surveys were completed. All figures rounded to the nearest whole number. Results of the survey are available upon request from wholebabysurvey@wholefoods.com.

Think about these findings. More women cited money as a greater fear than their baby's health. Balancing work and child rearing was more daunting to them than possessing adequate parenting skills. Shocking? Not at all! People rarely talk openly about their financial issues, and when they do, it is often when their options have run dry and they're desperate. If this book does anything, I hope it will inspire you to address your money concerns, whatever they may be, both early and sensibly.

ON YOUR MARK, GET SET, GO!
YOUR PERSONAL STARTING POINT

Before you can start, you're going to have to know where your finances are at this moment. That may mean swallowing a strong dose of reality, not something many people particularly relish but a critical first step. You'll need to take a hard, analytical look at what you've done with your money up to this point. After all, where you are today is the result of a lifetime's worth of choices, and knowing what got you to this stage will help you to determine what you need to do now to achieve your goals. It doesn't matter what you have or don't have today; what matters is where you want your growing family to be.

Let's begin with your personal starting point. Visualize a line in the sand: this is your current financial situation. Now, picture a series of finish lines at various points in the distance. Those are your goals. If you don't have specific goals yet, that's okay; you will, and this book will help you to identify, prioritize, and achieve them. Your expanding family may inspire you to buy a home that is roomy enough for you all, plan for fun vacations, or save for college and retirement. The possibilities are as boundless as your dreams, and now is the time to start putting together a plan to achieve them.

If you're currently in debt, you may be several paces behind where you want to be; if you own more than you owe, you may be ahead. Wherever you are now, accept it as your starting point. As long as you are focused on moving in a positive direction, not wasting time and money by running around in circles, you're on the right track. There may be times when you go backwards—the old "two steps forward, one step back" rule applies to finance, too. Everybody makes mistakes, and even the best, wisest, and most learned financial planners lose track of bills or overspend from time to time. What's crucial is that you learn from your financial missteps so you can avoid making them over and over again.

You will know where you are on this imaginary starting line by completing the net worth statement and liability worksheets on the following pages. These will give you a good sense of where you are right now and help you figure out what you need to do to get where you want to be. Many people only have a vague idea about what is going on with their finances. You may not know how much you have in your checking account, much less in a retirement account or other investments. Don't let this stop you from doing the exercise! Exact numbers are ideal, but if you don't have them right now, then give it your best conservative estimate. You can always go back and be more precise later.

As you go through these worksheets, account for everything in detail. You may be surprised at how much you actually own (and owe). It is easy to forget about certain key items, so move slowly and carefully. Begin with your net worth statement, assets first (Figure 1.1).

Next, analyze your liabilities, or what you currently owe (Figure 1.2). This can be an intimidating task, but you've got to face it eventually so plunge in now. Most people find this exercise quite cathartic, and it is yet another positive step forward along the path to achieving your financial goals.

After you know how much you have and how much you owe, it's time for the moment of truth: calculating your net worth. After completing your net worth and liability worksheet, use the formula below to determine the precise amount.

Total Asset Value – Total Liabilities = Net Worth

That wasn't too bad, was it? If you're like most people, you may be surprised at how much you actually own or owe. It can be amazing how much we accumulate over the years! Now you know your net worth—your personal starting point.

The last step in this chapter is to complete the following cash flow worksheets to learn where you are currently spending your money. This

Figure 1.1 *Net Worth Statement Worksheet*

NET WORTH STATEMENT WORKSHEET	
Asset	**Value**
Cash in Savings Accounts	
Cash in Checking Accounts	
Certificates of Deposit (CDs)	
Cash on Hand	
Money Market Accounts	
Money Owed to Me	
Cash Value of Life Insurance	
Savings Bonds	
Stocks	
Bonds	
Mutual Funds	
Vested Value of Stock Options	
Other Investments	
Individual Retirement Accounts (IRAs)	
Keogh Accounts	
401(k) or 403(b) Accounts	
Other Retirement Plans	
Market Value of Your Home	
Market Value of Other Real Estate	
Blue Book Value of Cars/Trucks	
Boats, Planes, Other Vehicles	
Jewelry	
Collectibles	
Furnishings and Other Personal Property	
Other	
Total Asset Value:	

doesn't entail designing a comprehensive budget, which comes later in the book when you know more about your total financial picture and what you need or want to add in and take out. Right now, all you need to

Figure 1.2 *Liability Worksheet*

LIABILITY WORKSHEET	
Liability	**Value**
Mortgages	
Car Loans	
Bank Loans	
Student Loans	
Home Equity Loans	
Other Loans	
Credit Card Balances	
Real Estate Taxes Owed	
Income Taxes Owed	
Other Taxes Owed	
Other Debts	
Total Liabilities:	

know is what your current cash flow situation looks like, so you can see where you're spending today and on what and how much you have left over for savings.

Begin by calculating your monthly income. Complete the following monthly income worksheet chart (Figure 1.3) by filling in any income source relevant to you, then calculate the total by finding the sum of all of your monthly income sources. It is important to know your gross income, but your net pay, which is your gross pay minus taxes, is the figure you'll need for this exercise. Be sure to include monthly averages for any variable income you may receive, such as commissions, as well as occasional income influxes like large tax refunds or bonuses.

Now, let's figure out where all of that cash going. Find out by completing the following monthly expenses worksheet (Figure 1.4). Because many of these expenses are variable, such as utilities and groceries, it is important to average them when calculating the monthly amount. Don't forget to include periodic expenses, such as insurance premiums or vehicle registration fees.

Figure 1.3 *Monthly Income Worksheet*

MONTHLY INCOME WORKSHEET	
Income Source	**Amount**
Employer 1	
Employer 2	
Retirement/Pension	
Child Support	
Spousal Support/Alimony	
Social Security	
Government Benefits	
Unemployment Insurance	
Other	
Other	
Total Monthly Income:	

After completing the monthly income and monthly expense worksheets, use the following equation to calculate your cash flow.

Total Monthly Expenses – Total Monthly Income = Cash Flow

Once you've calculated your cash flow, you are aware of how much (or, in some cases, how little) you have to work with at the moment. I cannot stress enough just how critical these simple exercises really are. If ever you needed clarity in your life, this is the time, and understanding your net worth and cash flow represents a real moment of truth. It answers the main question of this chapter: Where are you now? With this information, you can transform your life. That's real power, and it's in your hands.

Once you've determined where you are financially, you're a big step closer to understanding how far you need to go to achieve your goals and protect your family's future. There will be challenges along the way, but by staying focused and motivated, you can conquer them. Use the time-tested strategies and advice in this book to help you overcome the wide variety of economic difficulties and stressors you may encounter. Consider this your personal financial tool kit, complete with everything you'll need to build the life you want for your growing family.

Figure 1.4 *Monthly Expenses Worksheet*

MONTHLY EXPENSES WORKSHEET	
Source	**Amount**
Housing	
Rent/Mortgage	
2nd Mortgage/Equity Line	
Condo Fees/HOA Dues	
Property Taxes	
Homeowners'/Renter's Insurance	
Time-shares	
Gas/Electric	
Property/Land	
Water/Sewer/Garbage	
Cable/Satellite	
Telephone	
Other Housing Expenses	
Home Care	
Maintenance/Cleaning	
Pool Service/Gardening	
Monitored Alarm	
Pet Expenses	
Cell Phone/Pager	
Banking Fees/Postage	
Household Items	
Internet Service	
Other Home Care Expenses	
Food	
Groceries	
Dining Out	
At Work/School	
Other Food Expenses	
Medical	
Health/Dental Insurance	
Prescriptions	

(continued)

Figure 1.4 *Monthly Expenses Worksheet (continued)*

Source	Amount
Doctor's Visits	
Other Medical Expenses	
Transportation	
Vehicle Payment #1	
Vehicle Payment #2	
Gasoline	
Maintenance/Repairs	
Insurance	
Registration	
Tolls/Parking	
Public Transportation	
Other Transportation Expenses	
Clothing	
Clothing	
Jewelry	
Accessories	
Laundry/Dry Cleaning	
Other Clothing Expenses	
Education	
Tuition	
Lessons	
Materials	
Other Education Expenses	
Personal Care	
Haircuts/Color	
Cosmetics	
Manicures/Pedicures	
Spa Treatments	
Other Personal Care Expenses	
Entertainment	
Movies/Video	
Dining Out	
Sports/Hobbies/Clubs	

Figure 1.4 *Monthly Expenses Worksheet (continued)*

Source	Amount
Vacation/Travel	
CD/Tapes/Videos/DVD	
Books/Magazines	
Other Entertainment Expenses	
Unsecured Debt	
Credit/Charge Cards	
Bank/Credit Union Loans	
Medical Debt	
Student Loans	
Personal Loans	
Other Debt	
Miscellaneous	
Taxes	
Life Insurance	
Union Dues	
Storage Fees	
Cigarettes/Alcohol	
Gifts	
Religious/Charitable Contributions	
Other Miscellaneous	
Total Monthly Expenses:	

CHAPTER SUMMARY

- Recognize that there is no better time than now, before your baby is born or while he is very young, to get your finances in order.
- You can use your heightened emotions, both the negative and the positive, to your advantage.
- Remember not just the importance of financial security but also what it means: that you can take care of yourself no matter the emergency and prepare for all the enjoyable aspects of life.

- Find out just how financially secure you are at this point.
- If you have money troubles now, you may feel alone, yet this is a struggle you share with millions.
- Determine where you stand today—your personal starting point—by completing a net worth and cash flow statement.
- Figuring out where you are is a crucial first step towards getting where you want to be.

Chapter 2

The Meaning of Money

Understanding and Refining Your Values

WHAT DOES MONEY MEAN to you—and why should you be so focused on it at this time in your life? The answer is simple: a new baby comes with a whole new set of financial concerns. You're going to be making many key decisions, both now and in the future, and your perception of money has a direct impact on your spending and saving habits. If you want to get the most out of every penny, then you must first understand and define your financial philosophy. After all, action follows attitude, not the reverse.

Unfortunately, many people fail to think about money as anything more than a means to an end—go to work, get paid, go shopping, and so on. They have no real financial plan and give very little thought beyond what bills need to be dealt with immediately or what new things might be great to own. This monetary shortsightedness can have significant consequences for their ability to improve their financial situation, plan for the future, and achieve their financial goals.

Without careful consideration of how and where you spend your money, you get wasted dollars today and jeopardized goals over the long term. Thus, gaining clarity on what money means to you is essential to making smart, well-considered decisions that will enhance your family's short- and long-term happiness. The income you receive in exchange for our hard work and effort deserves your utmost respect and the harder you have to work for your paycheck, the more preciously you should treat each cent.

Right now, while you are in the process of having a baby or your child is very young, is the perfect opportunity to think about what money means to you and to refine your financial values. One of the most exciting aspects of pregnancy and new parenthood is the knowledge that anything is possible. Your baby has every opportunity available to her, and you have the ability to ensure that she is not only raised in a secure environment but that one day her financial dreams can be achieved.

PAYCHECK PAYBACK

One of the things that always fascinated me during my counseling years was the number of people who would come to see me, distraught and despondent about the chaotic state of their financial affairs, while grasping a stack of bills in one hand and several shopping bags in another. It wouldn't be long before I'd learn exactly how much money was coming in and what was going out each month—and on what.

All too often, there was a tremendous disconnect as to *why* their financial woes were worsening. For the most part, these were not people who had lost their job or who had experienced some unfortunate, uncontrollable setback, although there were plenty of individuals in this situation. A good portion of my clients had simply adopted a toxic financial philosophy. Their spending and saving attitudes and habits needed a serious overhaul. They'd usually spend whatever money was coming in as quickly as they could and on things that made them feel good at that moment. They felt an uncontrollable urge to buy and a hunger for the immediate, though fleeting, gratification that comes from frivolous spending. For many of my clients, saving was inconceivable, if not impossible. "On my paycheck? No way!" I heard time and time again.

Tragically, many in this situation worked long hours for every dime they made, some earning minimum wage or just above. What was the reason behind their negative spending habits? Often, they were "getting back" at their nine-to-five jobs by spending money haphazardly, impulsively, and on material things that would create a feeling of wealth. Their philosophy was: "I work so hard, for so many hours, doing things I don't particularly like. My boss doesn't value me, and I have to bend over backwards . . . it's ME time now." It was as if they were taking revenge on the money they made and on the fact that others are able to live the good life. Unfortunately, in the end, the only people they hurt were themselves.

If this sounds at all familiar, you must break this pattern of destructive behavior. Stop abusing your money. Beating it up won't make it behave, but it will make it disappear. Now that there's a new baby depending on you, it's more important than ever that you adopt a healthier financial philosophy and set of behaviors.

WHY PARENTS HAVE TO BE EXTRA CAREFUL

Many new parents find it remarkably easy to put financial common sense on the back burner and get caught up in shopping for all the tempting new baby products on the market. They purchase items they cannot really afford for all the wrong reasons.

What are the wrong reasons? Well, many parents buy their children things out of guilt. Maybe you have to work and can't spend as much time with your baby as you'd like, or maybe you are so tired and grumpy towards the baby that you buy something cute to ease your sense of remorse. Other "wrong" reasons include trying to keep up with your neighbors or friends who may have more money than you have or arming yourself with luxury baby goods so you seem outwardly successful, even if your income really can't support it. Wherever these types of feelings come from, compensating with a "thing" offers only a temporary reward, and it doesn't solve the underlying issue. Moreover, because the money to buy these items often puts you in even more serious financial peril, in the long run, this behavior often has a serious detrimental effect.

It is imperative that you understand your inner motivations to earn, spend, and save so you can make the best choices for you and your family. Most of the time, those pesky urges to spend recklessly can get us into real trouble. Impulsive decisions often lack the careful, rational thought process that considered decisions entail, and they are rarely a good place from which to make fundamental decisions. If your child's welfare is at all important to you, there is simply no more appropriate or important time than now to understand what money means to you and to refine your attitude and behavior so that you make sound economic choices.

Very often, all it takes is to step back for a moment when you're about to make a purchase and think carefully, giving thorough consideration to the issue of what you want versus what you need. For example, let's say you are buying a stroller. While at the store, you see the accessory package that goes along with it, which you certainly did not plan on getting—in fact, it's an additional $85. Yes, a detachable rain cover and cup holder can be useful, but they may not be the best use of your money right now. Every baby store and infant department in America stocks countless "add-on" impulse items like these, which are remarkably easy to throw casually into your cart. Picking up a few unplanned items along the way may not seem like a big deal, but when you reach the cash register, you see just how quickly it all adds up.

Anxieties over money concerns are not only common but tend to magnify during pregnancy and new parenthood. This is a time when conflicting desires and financial realities tear at families. If you are among the vast number of Americans who are living paycheck to paycheck (about 41 percent of workers, according to a 2006 CareerBuilder.com survey), and with the average cost to raise a newborn around $10,000 the first year, it can be very difficult to figure out how to squeeze that extra money out of an already strained budget. On the other hand, you also most likely have the very common desire to get out there and shop for your new baby and, stress be darned, get whatever stroller *du jour* is on the market. However remember: How you choose to behave right now directly affects your future, and the cost of making a wrong decision at this time in your life can be high.

YOUR FINANCIALLY HEALTHY DREAM CHILD

What are your goals for your child's future financial well-being? How would you like your child to deal with monetary issues when he is grown? Nearly every parent I have worked with has expressed the same desire: "I don't want her to make the same mistakes as I did!" While it is not realistic to expect to raise a child who *never* makes a bad financial decision, you absolutely can be a positive influence in his life and help him to avoid destructive behavior patterns and major financial pitfalls. The sooner you start thinking about these issues, the better.

Think about your baby and money. When she is grown, do you want her to:

- ☐ Adapt to financial change easily?
- ☐ Be charitable?
- ☐ Appreciate what he is given rather than expecting more?
- ☐ Work in a profession out of love and passion, rather than just doing it for the money?
- ☐ Be a savvy shopper?
- ☐ Enjoy what money can bring, rather than fear the absence of it?
- ☐ Plan effectively for the future?
- ☐ Be financially honest?
- ☐ If necessary, know how to take financial assistance graciously?
- ☐ Recognize the importance of hard work?
- ☐ Be able to discuss money rationally?
- ☐ Know her value in the workforce and be able to negotiate a salary with confidence?
- ☐ Be self-sufficient?
- ☐ Believe that you can't buy happiness?
- ☐ Have an overall positive attitude about money?

You answered yes to all of these questions, didn't you? Of course you did: this is not just your financially healthy dream child—it's pretty much all of ours. Think about it, isn't this everything you would like to be as well?

You can vastly improve the chances of your child possessing these attributes if you have them. So let's get *you* there first! Healthy financial values are taught by way of not only active instruction but also observation. In other words, if you engage in positive financial behaviors, your child will see that and at least come away with that experience as a foundation for good financial health.

LOOKING BACK—AND MOVING FORWARD

Your parents, or whoever raised you, were instrumental in developing your attitudes about money—just as you will be with your child. To appreciate fully the impact that your financial values will have on your child, it would be beneficial to take a look back and review your own upbringing. You're likely to find plenty of clues as to why you have the financial values you do, including those you want to pass along and those you'd rather get rid of fast.

My own childhood is a perfect example. I certainly adopted many of my financial habits from my parents, several of which were unhealthy and I had to learn to break. My mother, as much as I would have liked her to be at the time, was by no stretch of the imagination the cardigan- and pearl-wearing type. She was a war-protesting, circle-sharing (this was the early 1970s, mind you), highly unconventional young mother of seven children. However, her financial attitudes and actions were absolutely conservative: take few risks and save as much as possible.

On the other side of the spectrum was my father. He was impetuous and believed that money was to be made fast, big, and by taking huge risks. He also thought it should be spent on whatever you want; hence the two-seated sports car he drove up our driveway in one day, which my mother promptly made him return.

Ultimately, as I developed my own attitudes towards money, I had to make some decisions about these often conflicting perspectives. Some worked well; others didn't. For example, I used to avoid investing my earnings because it felt too much like gambling, choosing instead to tuck every dollar I made into a low-interest (but perfectly safe) savings account. However, after really looking at the numbers and learning the facts about the stock market, I eventually changed and began cautiously to invest. It wasn't long before my money began to grow rather than stagnate. I moved past my aversion to putting my money at risk through research and learning. You can, too. Think about your own upbringing carefully and at length. Consider the financial values that your parents conveyed to you and whether or not you took them on as your own:

- In general, what money messages did you get from them?
- What did you experience regarding money? Was there fear, anxiety, or stress?
- Did they say one thing about money but do another?
- Did they save money, and if so, did they talk about it?
- Did they discuss household bills and what things cost?
- How did they feel about people who had less/more than they did?
- What made you happy about the way they treated money—and what upset you?
- Was there ever a sense that there should be more money or that they deserved more?
- Did they talk about money in a positive or negative way—if at all?
- What was the best money message you got out of them— and the worst?

Whatever your thoughts and recollections are, one thing should be clear: your parental role models influence your behavior. What they did, said, and felt about money was in some way translated back to you, and you either took their values on as your own or you rejected them. The choice is yours:

- **Accept it.** As a parent, you will be passing on a myriad of principles, and financial values are most definitely among them. Just as your parents taught you what money was about, whether actively or passively, so too will you be passing these values on to your child. What legacy do you want to pass on? This is not to say that your child will take everything you say as gospel and be a little clone of you, just that you do have incredible influence and you should not take that lightly.

- **Change it.** You are in an incredible position of power. There is not a more ideal time than now to change your financial value system for the better. Whatever your perception of what money is right now, you can make it even better. Just by giving this issue serious thought and making decisions based on what values you want to instill in your child, you are putting yourself in a good position to make a huge difference in how *both* you and your child will think about money.

KNOW YOUR VALUES AND ACHIEVE YOUR GOALS

Getting a handle on your financial values is an important step towards being able to achieve your goals. It will also help you prioritize your objectives, a key step in financial planning. Sure, you may be able to work longer hours, get a part-time job, or ask for a raise—all totally valid options that I will address more fully later on—but very often the area over which we have the most control is our budget. Remember, the amount of money that is coming in each month is a finite sum, and you should do your best to make each dollar count.

When it comes to your child, what items are at the top of your priority list and why? Do you want to pay extra for a private nanny? If so, why? Would you rather spend the money on saving for your child's long-term education? If so, why? Do you want to be able to lavish him with toys and books and other things that will amuse him? If so, why? Always question and evaluate your purchases *before* you get to the cash register. If you don't, you just may think that you *can* have it all. Spending money on things that really don't fit in with a healthy value system is easy to do if you aren't analytical. Unless your resources are truly unlimited, impulsive spending will put you on shaky ground.

Financial missteps are a part of life, and shopping for your new baby is no exception. You'll more than likely make some mistakes and have regrets. You may look back and wonder: what was I thinking when I bought that $80 stuffed unicorn for my child? Again, what's crucial is how you react to your mistakes. Never forget that we can often learn valuable lessons from them. Do so, and when your child is growing up, you will be more likely to forgive her errors, provided she can learn and grow from them, too. Try not to obsess or overanalyze this issue; just make a point of treating your money respectfully, because you or your partner worked hard for it.

It's also important to remember not to beat yourself up over each extravagant purchase—you're human, and resisting every single desire is not only impossible but also unhealthy. A life without the occasional splurge is no fun.

When you're thinking about making a purchase, you can reduce waste by considering a few internal questions:

- Why am I buying this?
- What is it really going to do for me?
- Do I need it?
- Can I afford it?
- Would my money be better spent on something else?

WHAT *ARE* YOUR MONEY VALUES?

Let's assume you have an extra $100 in your budget every month. Where would you most likely put it? Use the following desire-or-require worksheet to help you prioritize your goals (Figure 2.1). First, decide if the items in each expense category represent things you desire or things you require and put a check mark in the appropriate column. Then, rank the categories in both columns according to where you would most like to put the $100.

After you finish, think about what things matter most to you right now. What do you most desire, and what do you most require? Chances are, they'll be pretty different. They'll likely change over time as well. Remember, your priorities today are not necessarily your priorities tomorrow. It's important to know what they are now so you can strike a balance between what you want and what you need. If you would love to put the $100 per month toward your personal care, for example, but paying off your credit card debt is more pressing, begin to consider how you can do a bit of both, maybe $70 to the cards, and $30 to the spa. Thinking about these sorts of issues now will help you develop an effective personal family budget, which you'll complete at the end of this book.

Figure 2.1 *Desire-or-Require Worksheet*

DESIRE-OR-REQUIRE WORKSHEET			
Desire	Require	Rank	Expense Category
			Home: Decorating or improving your current home, saving for a new or larger home
			Food: Buying better, more exotic, or organic groceries; dining out, going out for lunch, coffee drinks, and snacks
			Health Care: Adding or increasing health/ dental insurance, buying vitamins or other health-related products and services, therapy/ counseling, gym membership
			Transportation: Buying a second or better vehicle, maintaining or improving your current vehicle
			Travel: Taking weekend trips, cruises, camping, vacations
			Clothing: Buying more or nicer clothes and accessories for you and your family
			Education: Enrolling in classes for you and or for other family members
			Personal Care: Getting haircuts, cosmetics, manicures and pedicures, spa treatments
			Entertainment: Spending on movies, reading material, music, hobbies, sporting events
			Unsecured Debt: Paying off credit and charge cards, loans, medical debt
			Gifts: Flowers, presents, or money for friends and family
			Charity: Making contributions to an organization, religious affiliation, or school
			Savings and Investing: Adding to any savings or investment account, including retirement and college funding
			Child Care: Babysitters, nannies, or other caregiver
			Baby Items: Purchasing toys, gear, gadgets, decorations, etc.

The bottom line is that you've got to know what is important to you and why. When I used to counsel people, I'd often push a completed budget back to a client and have them identify and circle the expenses that they really loved. I'd then say, "These are the areas we won't touch, OK? We'll consider them sacred unless we absolutely have to look at them to trim." The look of relief on their faces was amazing. In the end, most found they were able to keep spending some of their money on the things they truly valued, while still improving their overall financial situation by reducing or eliminating those things that were of lesser importance. This is what you can do, too, once you know what you value.

WHAT IS YOUR MONEY ATTITUDE?

Taking the following money attitude quiz will help you assess your thoughts about money. Answer each of the following questions with a "yes" or "no", depending on how you feel about the statement.

QUIZ: Money Attitude

1. The fact that others have more money than I do depresses me.
2. I deserve more money than I have.
3. It is fine to use credit to get what I want, even if I have trouble repaying the balance.
4. I worry about money, even when I have enough to pay my bills and save for goals.
5. Shopping in sales racks and discount stores makes me feel like a loser.
6. When I buy nice things, I feel like a success.
7. I find it difficult to part with money, even for important expenses.
8. I feel better when I am spending money than when I am saving it.
9. Money controls me rather than the other way around.
10. I judge others for what they have or don't have.
11. I can't take a handout even if I need the money.
12. I don't think it's right to discuss—or even think about—money too much.

Count the number of "yes" responses you made, and for each one, ask yourself the following:

- Would I like to change the way I feel about this attitude?
- Is my attitude a reaction to something that happened, or is happening, in my life?
- Can I pinpoint where that attitude comes from?

Your money values have a direct effect on the way you treat money today and determine your financial goals for tomorrow. Remember, your money attitudes are not carved in stone. They are flexible and can be adjusted to meet your fluctuating needs. If you want to fine-tune them, you can. Take action to turn the situation around.

There's an old joke that really captures this situation, How many psychiatrists does it take to change a lightbulb? Only one—but the lightbulb has to *want* to change.

RULES TO LIVE BY

While each one of us has a unique perspective on money, a few general values and perspectives are good for just about everyone to possess. After working with thousands of people over the years, I have witnessed the same mistakes being made repeatedly by my clients. While personally making and learning from them can be useful, why not save a bit of time and cash by learning from others as well?

Treat Every Incoming Dollar Respectfully

Almost no one can afford to waste money, yet it happens all the time. As a new parent, you may be overwhelmed by the vast array of items available on the baby market today, and you may not be behaving as carefully with your spending as you should be. It is not uncommon for new parents to buy far more than their baby will ever really need or use. By treating money with respect—shopping according to your refined, well-considered values and not frittering it away on things that you don't really care about or need or that simply don't make sound financial sense—you can make your money stretch enough to meet your goals. Consider each potential purchase closely, taking into account how long it took you to earn the cash for the price. If your net hourly wage is $22 per hour and the crib you want to buy is $350, it would take you nearly 16 hours to pay for it. Use that information to decide if it's worth it.

Avoid the Entitlement Trap

No parent wants an "entitled" child (one who appreciates nothing but expects everything and more). Of course, your baby is precious and it's only natural to want to shower him with the finest things that money can buy. I am a parent, too, and I am fully aware of the temptation to splurge and ignore the fact that such overspending may force you to compromise on other necessary expenses and goals. Think about the message you are sending. One day, you will want your child to be grateful for the gifts she receives (and much later on, to work hard for the salary she makes) and not think that it is her birthright to live a life of privilege. You also want your child to be able to prioritize and have healthy financial values. Remember, you will be your child's first financial role model, so be careful that your behavior reflects the messages you want to send.

Value Your Work

It is vital that you teach your child that all work is honorable. This cannot happen without having a great attitude about your own employment decisions. No matter where your money comes from, whether from a minimum wage or transitional job, a career you've trained your whole life for, or being a stay-at-home parent, all work has intrinsic value. Anytime you make an economic decision for the ultimate good of you and your family, you should be proud of yourself. If you adopt and convey a sense of pride in what you do, you will teach your kids to have a similar positive outlook.

Have Great Expectations

Your little one won't be little forever. Think big for him, for you, and for your entire family. Expect that you can repay all of your debt and never owe money to creditors again. You can do that by changing your perspective about borrowing, becoming more informed about how credit works, and planning for the future. Know that you can resist the temptations to overspend, and that you can stay true to your real fiscal needs and desires. Believe that you can downsize when necessary and still live happily. Think big, think grand, and take decisive action to make it happen. This is not just a new life you are raising; it's a fresh start for all of you!

Consider Yourself a Contributor

You may notice that throughout this book, I never use the word *consumers* when referencing individuals. While this term is important to economists, the media, and financial organizations dedicated to product and service advocacy (consumer unions, consumer reports, etc.), defining yourself this way is problematic and even harmful. After all, we do so much more than *consume*. We are also earners, givers, savers, and investors. Sadly, no single word adequately describes us as members of society who do all these positive things with our money. Reducing our self-definition to a single word, such as *consumer,* is not just troubling but destructive as well. It means we are nothing more than *users*. As a parent, you do not want your child to be someone who only takes. You want her also to add value to the world. Therefore, it pays to redefine ourselves not as mere consumers but as *contributors* instead.

There are extraordinary benefits to having an informed and comprehensive understanding of money. For starters, you'll learn much more about who you are and what you want out of life, which is always wonderful. Furthermore, because your attitude about money drives your earning, spending, and saving behaviors, getting a clearer picture of what they are and where they come from will help you make better, more thoughtful, and more powerful financial decisions. Finally, you will be passing your outlook on money matters to your child. In all my years of helping people with their economic concerns, no one has ever walked away after analyzing their thoughts about money without gaining a better, more focused plan for their future. Healthy financial values are an invaluable gift to give your child.

Whatever money means to you, know one thing: that it's not just a means to an end—it's a beginning.

CHAPTER SUMMARY

- Recognize that as a new parent, you have increased financial pressures to contend with.
- Think about how you want your child to grow up thinking about money and refine the attitudes and behaviors you want to pass on to him.
- Understand how your own upbringing affects the way you think about and deal with money and commit to changing the negative thoughts and habits you want to stop.
- Seek and strike a balance between what you desire and what you require.
- Understand your financial values so you can prioritize your expenses and goals.
- Remember the rules to live by:
  o Treat your money with great respect
  o Expand your self-definition from consumer to contributor
  o Avoid the entitlement trap
  o Value your work, whatever it may be
  o Expect great things out of your money and your abilities

Chapter 3

The Dangers of Debt

Avoiding Financial Traps and Pitfalls

A LL TOO MANY AMERICANS are holding on to overwhelming consumer debt. As of this writing, the average U.S. credit card–carrying household owes nearly $9,000, and there's no sign of a slowdown anytime soon. If that sum doesn't sound daunting enough, consider the fact that it's nearly one-third of the average citizen's annual income, which, according to 2005 U.S. census bureau statistics, is approximately $35,500. Moreover, that's just unsecured credit; which doesn't include other types of debt such as mortgages, vehicle loans, and student loans. However, whether you owe more or less than the national average (or than your friends and neighbors), spending beyond your means and borrowing to make up the difference is the quickest way to destroy the very thing you are trying to create for your growing family: real, lasting financial security.

Figure 3.1 *Consumer Debt Graph*

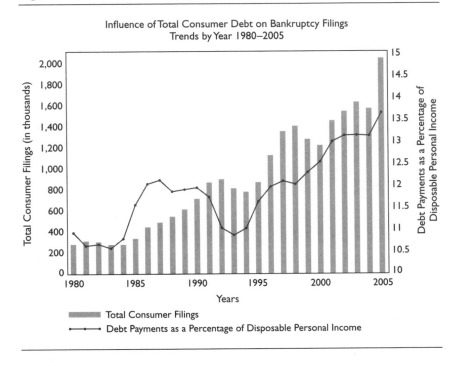

Influence of Total Consumer Debt on Bankruptcy Filings
Trends by Year 1980–2005

Total Consumer Filings
Debt Payments as a Percentage of Disposable Personal Income

Research by the Federal Reserve Board indicates that household debt is at a record high relative to disposable income (Figure 3.1).

If you've been living in the negative each month by spending more than you earn, know that the time has come to say no more, enough is enough. The health and welfare of your new baby is the perfect incentive to take some positive steps in your life. This means spending within your means and saving for future expenses and goals. Because paying down debt and using credit wisely is so important, it should be at the very top of every family's financial priority list.

What if you aren't in debt? That's terrific. Keep it that way, by being aware of the internal and external influences that are working very hard to get you to get reckless with your money right now. This includes everything from wanting to see your precious child in only the most expensive, top-of-the-line gear available to trying desperately to keep up with what other families have to giving in to the pressure to spend that's generated by marketers and retailers as they aggressively promote their products in new and enticing ways. It is important that you know how to resist overspending by keeping your economic realities in mind and to build a positive credit rating so you can achieve your financial goals at the lowest possible cost.

PERSPECTIVE MATTERS

How bad does debt have to get before you worry about it enough to take action? Some of my previous clients had come to me distraught beyond words because they owed $2,000 and it would take them eight months to repay it. Others came carrying a quarter of a million dollars in credit card debt, and it barely registered as a concern. Me? If I owe $20, I toss and turn all night. How high the balances have to climb before you do something about it depends on your individual financial situation and your ability to accept debt as a part of your life.

With debt, as with health, early intervention is the best practice. Your options with lenders and other creditors are almost always more varied and attractive if you contact them before you miss a payment. If you hide your head in the sand and hope it all goes away, you are doing nothing more than exposing the body part that will be kicked—repeatedly and with force!

THE REAL COST OF CREDIT

Let's say you owe a rather unpleasant $9,000 to your credit card company. How does that really affect your finances? Well, if the interest rate were an average 18 percent, the monthly finance charge would be around $135. No matter how much you make, that is a pretty substantial amount of money to burn. Consider what you could be doing with that $135 every month instead:

- Deposit it into a tax-deferred college savings plan for 17 years. If the average annual return were a conservative 7 percent, you'd save about $44,000 for your child's higher education costs.
- Return it to your budget to cover one or more of your household bills.

- Buy a nice pair of shoes for yourself. Everyone is entitled to an occasional indulgence!
- Splurge on a luxury item for your baby. Having a child is a wonderful time in your life, and you should enjoy it responsibly.
- Cover the cost of a babysitter and a meal out on the town.
- Enjoy a massage *and* a manicure and pedicure.
- Make a generous (and tax-deductible) charitable donation to an organization that supports a cause you really care about.

The point is that there are countless wonderful things, from the practical and necessary to the whimsical and discretionary, that you could be doing with that cash. I'm sure that you'll agree that contributing to a creditor's bottom line is not one of them.

COMING TO TERMS WITH DEBT

How did you get into debt in the first place? For many people, it was a slow but steady nosedive. You charged something, a suit for a job interview perhaps, and when the statement came in, you paid the balance in full. Then you charged more. However, rather than paying it all off, you paid half of what you owed and rolled the balance over to the following month. Soon, a modest $250 balance grew to $2,500. There was no way you could pay off thousands of dollars in one fell swoop *and* pay regular bills while still enjoying life, so you wrote a check for the minimum requested payment or perhaps a touch more.

Eventually, you noticed that the interest rate you were being charged was no longer in the single digits and very little of your payment was making a dent in the principal. Now you can't even remember what you spent all that money on anyway. Maybe it was a combination of things— a new crib, fancy baby clothes, tires for your car, and, well, probably a bunch of other stuff. Essentially, the balance came from using plastic to supplement your income, which isn't a good strategy. To make matters worse, because you have already sent a large chunk of change to your creditors last month, you have even less to work with, so you run out of cash sooner, and the cycle continues.

In many cases, the arrearage that people have gotten into was absolutely preventable. "Oh, no it wasn't," you may be thinking to yourself as you read this, "The debt was unavoidable." What would have happened if you had suffered through living within your means instead? Most likely, you'd have managed; you would have likely found a way to get by, and in the end you'd be a lot better off. Trust in your ability to make it through the hard times without having to borrow.

CHOOSING PLASTIC?

Are you thinking about opening a credit card account to help pay for new baby items? There are many types of credit cards out there, so choose carefully. You have a lot of options!

Secured Credit Card
With a secured credit card, you put down a certain amount of money, typically a few hundred dollars, as collateral. That secured sum is your credit line, and you use the card as you would any other credit card. Secured cards are excellent if you haven't developed a strong credit score yet or need to rebuild your credit. The issuing financial institution assumes little risk—it can always take the money if you default on paying—so almost anyone can get one. However, keep in mind that the annual fees tend to be higher than for unsecured cards.

General-Use Credit Card
These are your typical credit cards. They often have the Visa or MasterCard logo on them, but there are others, such as Discover Card. You can use them just about anywhere. While they aren't difficult to get, the cards with the best terms are only available to those with a positive credit history.

These cards come with either *variable* interest rates or *fixed* interest rates. There actually isn't much difference between the two for cardholders: variable rate cards are usually based on the prime lending rate or the London Interbank Offered Rate (LIBOR). These financial benchmarks are a few percentage points above what banks charge each other when making loans. The rates do go up and down, though typically not by much. The credit card application may read: "Prime + 3%." Therefore, if the prime rate is 8.25 percent, the adjusted prime rate (APR) would be 11.25 percent. A fixed-rate card won't have an interest rate that adjusts, but the initial interest rate may be a touch higher than that of the variable rate card. All in all, the difference is minimal.

Charge Card

The most common charge card is American Express. Instead of being able to maintain a revolving balance, which you can do with credit cards, you have to pay the entire sum you borrowed by the time the bill rolls in. In most cases, these cards come with substantial annual fees but can keep your spending in check because of the forced repayment time frame.

Rewards Credit Card

These are general-use credit cards with all sorts of goodies built in to them. By using the card to make purchases, you build up points that can go toward airline miles, tickets to sporting events, cash-back rewards, and other things you may want. Many cardholders never redeem the rewards at all, though. Keep in contact with the issuer (all it takes is a phone call) to know how much you've accumulated and what you can use it for.

Retailer's Credit Card

Almost all major stores offer their own credit card, which you can use at their store or group of stores only. The major benefit to having a retailer's card is if you shop there often, many stores offer cardholders access to special deals and sales. The only caveat with retailers' cards is that it is easy to apply for those you don't need—every time you walk into a store you're asked if you want to save 10–15 percent on the day's purchases by opening an account. Remember, having too much credit is an invitation to go overboard, and randomly applying for credit can hurt your score.

Affinity Credit Card

Affinity cards are similar to rewards cards, only the reward goes to the sponsored charity or organization, such as a nonprofit agency or university. When you use the card, the issuing bank donates a percentage of what you spend to the partnering organization. If you have a particular passion for a cause, this can be a nice way to give back.

Emergency *What?*

Ever hear of something called an "emergency credit card"? You may have one of these imaginary items in your wallet. If so, it's time to change its name. So-called emergency cards help millions of people get *into*—not out of—financial trouble. We now turn to plastic not just to make a convenient purchase but in times of real and true economic crisis.

All too often I have heard people deep in debt say that they need their credit cards to cover any financial emergencies that may arise. This makes absolutely no sense, especially if you are already in debt. After all, if you are already behind, borrowing more at even higher interest rates and finance fees is not going to help. Next month, the expected payment will be even higher. Where is that money going to come from? Charging when you are in financial trouble is like reaching for a leaky inner tube when you are drowning. It will keep you afloat for a moment, but it won't take long before you'll sink to the bottom of the pool.

Credit cards should be regarded as payment tools, nothing more. If you treat them as something else, whether it's a bonus to pay for holiday gifts, a vacation fund, or an "I'm not quite making it this month" account, than you are setting yourself up for financial failure. Right now, as a new or expecting parent, you no longer have the luxury to make these kinds of economic mistakes. Assuming that you really do want the best for your emerging family, recognize and accept that sometimes, doing without, even if it means making sacrifices, is a better decision in the long run than turning to credit cards to make ends meet.

If you'd like more information on the various types of credit cards available, I recommend that you check out Bankrate.com: *www.bankrate.com*. It maintains a comprehensive running list of available deals as well as a wealth of information on various borrowing issues.

PLANNING FOR DISASTER

Financial disasters absolutely and consistently happen. From job loss and income suspension to enormous medical bills and pipes bursting in your home, the list of potentially expensive disasters is long. Charging any of these mishaps to your credit card can certainly bail you out of the situation temporarily, but remember that it if you don't repay the balance as quickly as possible, you can get into serious money trouble. Credit cards should never be used as long-term financing.

While there's no such thing as an emergency credit card, there are emergency savings accounts and insurance policies that can protect your assets and save you from financial ruin. With the baby expenses you're currently handling, adding savings and insurance premiums into your budget may not feel possible, but with a bit of planning and a few changes, it usually can be done. When you construct your budget, look at all of your expenses and think of what you spend on cable, Internet access, entertainment, and other nonessentials. Isn't your financial security far more important than these luxuries? Prioritize and reroute the money you spend on less vital expenses to areas that build a reliable financial safety net.

HUMAN NATURE: THE GOOD AND THE BAD

One of the most common questions I am asked by both the media and my clients is "Why are people in so much debt?" While it would be great to have one clean, concise answer, it's not really possible; the issue is highly complex. There are many causes, from the skyrocketing cost of living to unstable wages, high housing costs, increasing interest rates, and much more. New parents have it even tougher because they must find a way to handle the costs of raising a child, often with less money coming into the household if one parent has to stay at home and care for the little one. However, after speaking with thousands of people, I've learned that a big reason why so many of us find our way into the black hole of debt is simple human nature. We hope for the best, and we fear the worst. In essence, our natural senses of optimism and pessimism can really work against us when it comes to borrowing.

The Issue With Optimism

The sense of hope and optimism that often accompanies the arrival of a new baby can transform even the most frugal and mall-phobic of us into the most enthusiastic of shoppers. A new baby is on the scene and you are excited! To heck with saving or scaling back when massive megastores and adorable boutiques are brimming with precious objects for your little one. You must have them all, so you charge all of it. You may even temporarily convince yourself that you'll figure out a way to pay it all off at some point in the future, right?

The truth is that such grand plans are hard to follow through on. This sort of inattentive charging can quickly spiral out of control if you aren't careful. Being overly confident with what you think you may be able to pay off at a future date may leave you facing a large amount of credit card debt. Once you've got it, you'll likely have a very difficult time getting out from under it.

If this pattern sounds familiar, start to switch over from an unrealistically optimistic perspective to one that is more realistic. Make sure not to be overly hopeful that you can charge today and pay tomorrow if it isn't a credible plan. Examine your cash flow in detail before adding to your credit card debt so you don't overdo it.

The Problem With Pessimism

I once overheard a new mother give advice to a pregnant woman: "Debt is just part of being a new parent. Get used to it now. When your baby is born, it's going to get worse."

I can't imagine a more defeatist and erroneous attitude. Debt is unavoidable? That is simply not true. Just because it is not uncommon to live with the burden of debt doesn't make it okay. This is not a condemnation of anyone who is currently in debt. I understand how easy it is to get behind, and I'm familiar with all of the reasons and circumstances. Nevertheless, it doesn't have to define the rest of your life.

In my experience, the number one reason why people fall into debt is due to some sort of income reduction, followed closely by overwhelming medical bills and divorce issues. Yes, these are major financial setbacks, but you can protect yourself from them, at least to some extent. The fact that at least one major financial hurdle will likely occur in your lifetime is reason enough actively to avoid debt and build up a substantial amount of savings. Remember, credit cards don't protect your family's future; you do.

Far too many people believe that the only way to make it and have what they need is to charge what they can't afford and worry about it later. Even worse is the prevalent belief that using credit cards to let them taste "the good life" is sensible and justifiable, when in reality it's just another way of robbing their family of true and lasting economic security.

YOUR CREDIT SCORE

Credit scores are mathematical models that help financial institutions and businesses make sound lending decisions. The most widely used is the FICO score, a model developed by the Fair Isaac Corporation. These scores range from a low of 300 to a high of 850. The higher your FICO is, the less expensive your loan may be. There is a lot of false information about these scores, though (for example, pulling your own credit report will not hurt your score), so be careful. Here is a breakdown of how your credit score is determined:

- **35%—Payment History:** How consistently you've paid you obligations matters most! Pay your debts on time, every time, to improve your credit score.
- **30%—Amounts Owed:** The less you owe the better, for your score and your wallet. Do your best to keep your balances well under the limit.
- **15%—Length of Credit History:** A long, positive history of borrowing and repaying money is favorable. Don't avoid credit; just use it responsibly.
- **10%—New Credit:** The number and type of credit inquiries you make can hurt your score. Only apply for accounts that you really need.
- **10%—Types of Credit Used:** Proving that you can handle all sorts of credit accounts looks good on your credit report. Try having a mix of a few credit cards, a loan, and a charge card. Remember to use them all responsibly!

KNOWLEDGE IS POWER

If ever there is a time to become an educated borrower, new parenthood is it. Here are the steps you can take to become one.

Read Your Credit Card Statement Carefully

Always review your credit card statement carefully and look for errors; they happen. Has your interest rate been increased? If you are holding on to some debt, see how much in finance fees you are being charged. Another reason to read your statement is to see the balance, which many people don't do because just looking at it is depressing! However, be brave; the only way to plan effectively for your financial future is to have an accurate idea of how much you owe and how far you need to go to eliminate debt from your life.

Ignore Those Free Checks

They arrive in the mail from your credit card company, are made out in your name, and all you have to do is deposit them into your checking account. You know the checks I'm referring to. However, they are essentially the same thing as cash advances, meaning interest accumulates immediately. I can't tell you how many times I heard clients say, "Of course I used them, they sent them to me!" and they then get angry with the credit card company. Save the aggravation and indignation—shred them as soon as they arrive.

Say No Thanks to Their Offer to Skip a Payment

This often happens right before or after the holiday season, when you are inspired to spend more money. While it can give you a sense of relief, interest is still being added to the balance, and you're not working down the principal. In the long run, this benefits the credit company, not you.

Reject Offers to Increase Your Credit Line

Do you *really* need to borrow $100,000? Massive credit lines lead to overcharging like nothing else. It's like a luscious chocolate cake sitting in a dieter's refrigerator. How do you resist? It's best if you don't have the cake there in the first place.

Reconsider the Products Offered

Credit card protection and insurance are cash cows for creditors. The Fair Credit Billing Act protects you against theft if you report the crime in a reasonable amount of time and limits your liability to $50, making paying for the extra protection redundant. Credit insurance is usually a mix of life, disability, and unemployment coverage. It is intended to cover your minimum monthly payment in the event that you lose your job or become disabled. A normal premium on a monthly balance of $4,000 would cost $30. Over the course of a year, the total is $360—money that is often better spent on a disability or term life insurance policy. In short, I've never seen credit insurance work well for anyone and do not recommend it.

The Cost of Time

The finance charges for carrying over credit card debt can be staggering. A typical, nonpunitive APR is around 15 percent. Look at the numbers and decide for yourself.

For example, say you charged a total of $3,000 on everything you want for baby to a credit card with a 15 percent interest rate. If you repay the balance over six months, paying just over $500 each month, the total finance charges will be around $117. If you repay the balance over two years, with a monthly payment of about $145, the finance charges will total around $495. Finally, if you make just the minimum payment (on average, about 2.5 percent of the monthly balance) until it is repaid, it would take you over 13 years to repay and cost over $2,515 in interest charges. In other words, your child will be well into puberty by the time you finish paying off the bassinette.

FORGE A POWERFUL RELATIONSHIP WITH CREDIT

Consumer credit is huge business in the United States, and other countries are doing their best to catch up. According to the Federal Reserve Board, Americans owed a total of roughly $2.4 trillion dollars in unsecured consumer debt in 2006. As a new parent, can you make credit cards profitable for you? Yes, but it takes work on your part. Most people *can* use credit to their advantage. If you always keep in mind that that bit of plastic is just a payment tool, you won't have to pay a penny in interest or finance charges. Many credit cards have extras built in that not only save you a lot of money but earn you cash and other goodies as well. These savings mean more money for baby and your entire family.

Using a credit card to pay for all the things you want for you and your baby can be a responsible option, as long as you repay the balance quickly. Immediately would be nice, but that's not always realistic. The key is to do it as soon as you are able. When you combine all the baby

MONITOR YOUR CREDIT REPORTS

Checking your credit report for accuracy and clearing up any errors is an integral part of good credit management. You may receive a free copy of your credit report from each of the three bureaus once a year from Annual Credit Report Request Service or directly from the credit bureaus listed below if you are unemployed or on public assistance or if your report is inaccurate due to fraud.

- Annual Credit Report Request Service
  P.O. Box 105281
  Atlanta, GA 30348-5281
  877-322-8228
  www.annualcreditreport.com

- Experian
  P.O. Box 2104
  Allen, TX 75013-2104
  888-397-3742
  www.experian.com

- TransUnion
  P.O. Box 390
  Springfield, PA 19064-0390
  800-916-8800
  www.transunion.com

- Equifax
  P.O. Box 105783
  Atlanta, GA 30348
  800-685-1111
  www.equifax.com

items you need or want—from diapers to decorations—the grand total can easily run in the thousands. However, under the right circumstances, using credit cards as a *short-term loan* and making a plan to repay it in fewer than six months, and doing so, can make sense. This is not contrary to the "payment tool" rule but a reminder that when used responsibly, credit cards can be utilized to your fiscal advantage.

When shopping for the things you need and want for your growing family, it is probably best to buy the big things, such as cribs and strollers, on credit. One of the greatest aspects of using credit cards for expensive purchases is the consumer protection they come with. The Fair Credit Billing Act ensures that you have the right to dispute charges for items or services that either never arrived, if you ordered them, or are deficient in some way. In other words, if the crib you ordered was missing a piece and the store you bought it from refuses to provide a refund or replacement, you can turn to the credit card company you used to pay for the item for relief.

GET OFF THE REVOLVING WHEEL OF DEBT

In the first chapter, you did an initial financial assessment. You calculated your net worth and completed a cash-flow statement to get a better understanding of your current position and how much debt you need to overcome to reach your goals. Now let's look at the details of that debt. Wouldn't you like to be debt-free before your baby is a toddler? In many cases you can. It just takes discipline and hard work. Remember, all good things in life require effort! Your baby certainly will. So why not put some effort into getting out from the crushing wheel of consumer debt?

Prioritize Your Debts

If you have multiple debts, the first thing you're going to have to do is to rank them in order of importance. This will help you to develop a realistic time line for eliminating each of them from your life. Complete the following debt prioritization worksheet (Figure 3.2) and mark off the debts you have, ranking each one according to its priority. Here are some helpful guidelines. Secured debts should come first because a legal judgment is not necessary to have the property taken away, then unsecured debts. After that, rank them according to interest rates; the more you are paying in finance charges, the more critical it is that you pay them off.

After completing the preliminary cash-flow statement in the first chapter, you now have a pretty good idea about how much money you have left to go toward your debts. Based on the ranking you gave each debt type, divide the money you have and attribute it to the accounts in order. That will be the amount you pay, even if the creditor accepts less.

Figure 3.2 *Debt Prioritization Worksheet*

DEBT PRIORITIZATION WORKSHEET						
Debt	Requested Monthly Payment	Interest Rate	Prepayment Penalty	Secured/Unsecured	Ranking	Revised Monthly Payment
Mortgages/ Home Equity Loans						
Vehicle Loans						
Student Loans						
Other Loans (consolidation, personal)						
Personal Loans*						
Real Estate Taxes Owed						
Income Taxes Owed						
Other Taxes Owed						
Other Debts (medical, collection accounts)						
Credit Card						
Credit Card						
Credit Card						
Credit Card						

*While personal loans (money you borrow from your friends and family) are really quite different from products sold by financial institutions, the debts you can incur this way can have a lasting impact on your personal life. Failure to pay them can ruin a relationship.

Be Realistic

The key to developing a good plan to eliminate your debt is to be realistic with what you can afford to pay each month. It's important not to underestimate your abilities or overcommit yourself. Your cash flow really does dictate what you can pay, so take the time to make sure it's accurate. For example, if your income is $2,000 a month but your expenses are $2,200, then you are overspending by $200, which will likely go on your credit cards and make matters worse. If your minimum payment due is $150 but you choose to double that, you will likely be short on funds again this month, with the deficit again going on the credit cards. Moreover, of course, as the debt grows, so do the finance charges, so you would have been better off making the minimum payment.

Suspend Charging

It does not make sense to repay the debt while you are still adding to the balance, so while you are in the period of repayment, do not use the cards at all anymore. It's all well and good to pay more than the minimum, but if you pull out the plastic when your cash dries up, you start to spin your wheels. Just about anyone with a checking account has a debit card, and I advise using that instead. You get many of the same benefits that credit cards offer, but you can't get into debt (although you can overdraw the account, so be careful).

Reduce the Interest Rates

Don't be afraid to pick up the phone and communicate with your creditors. If you have a long history with making your credit card payments on time, it is always worth asking for an interest rate reduction. Even if you have a spotty payment history, give it a try. It can't hurt. Getting the reduction will likely make a huge difference in your payback time and overall cost. Remember, all credit card companies are in the business to make money, and they want to keep your business. You may have had hard times in the past, but you could be a great customer in the future, so very often they want to treat you right. One caveat though: never make a promise you won't be able to keep. Always err on the conservative side.

Call the credit card company's customer service number and speak with a manager or supervisor. Explain that you have been a responsible customer and would like to continue doing business with them. Request an interest rate similar to the offer you are considering. Maintaining a relationship with the creditor you already have has its advantages: you don't have to begin again with a new company or monitor the date the deal ends. In addition, bouncing debt around with too many transfers can negatively impact your credit score because part of your score is determined by length of credit history.

Transfer Your Balances

Under certain circumstances, shifting your credit card debt to another issuer can be beneficial. For example, if your original creditor won't budge its 29 percent APR, but another is offering a 6 percent APR for one year, you'll save a lot of money in finance charges if you take the offer. However, there are factors to consider other than the math. If you tend to forget about paying bills and are charged late fees or are just "too busy" for careful money management, then balance transfers may not help you in the end. In many cases, just one late payment will cause the ultra-low interest rate on balance transfers to hike, not just on that card but all others, thanks to a little something called universal default.

To use these transactions effectively, you'll always have to be aware of due dates, make timely payments, and remember when the deal expires. Look for balance transfer offers with the lowest introductory interest rate for the longest amount of time, low post-introductory interest rate, no or low annual fees, and no or low balance-transfer fees (which can be up to 4 percent, equaling $200 on a $5,000 balance).

Transferring balances makes the most sense when you're certain you won't acquire more debt and will be concentrating on repaying what you owe. If you keep the old credit card open and use it to accumulate more debt, the benefit of the reduced interest rate is negated by the higher overall balance. Cancel or suspend use of the old card. Know, too, that you will likely be charged a high interest rate for purchases you make with the new card, so avoid racking up more debt on it as well.

Consolidation Loans

One of the most frequent questions people have when wanting to deal with their debt is: "Is taking out a consolidation loan the right thing for me?" This is when you take out a new loan to cover the balance of several accounts. The appeal of these loans is the money management factor—one account rather than many is convenient. The problem is that you will rarely be able to get such a loan that has an interest rate lower than what you already have. Oftentimes it is higher, which will make your debt even more expensive. Another issue associated with consolidation loans is that the cards with balances you just transferred to the loan are now empty and ready for use again. If you know you may use them and rebuild the balances (paint for the nursery, an adorable little baby outfit), close the cards immediately and stick to cash.

Debt Repayment Arrangements

An option that may be available to you is a debt repayment arrangement made through a credit counseling agency. These start with an initial financial counseling appointment, and if it makes sense for your individual situation, a three- to five-year repayment plan will be set up. Credit counseling agencies have established relationships with all the big and most of the small creditors and can often get your high interest rates lowered a bit. The real benefit, though, is that once you're on the plan, you agree to close your cards and not get into further debt for the duration of the arrangement. The plan is arranged only after you go through a detailed financial counseling session, so you know that you can afford to make the payments. A good agency will ensure that you set aside cash for savings as well, so you're prepared for emergencies and are saving to reach your goals.

I worked for Consumer Credit Counseling Service for many, many years. However, this doesn't make me any less objective. At this point, I've seen it all, from homeless clients to those making six-figure incomes and above, and you may be surprised by who needs help with their finances. Never feel ashamed to reach out to those who can offer guidance and assistance. Keep in mind that some agencies are definitely better than others. Do your research first by contacting the Better Business Bureau and checking for any registered complaints. Contact the National Foundation for Credit Counseling for information on an accredited agency in your area:

- National Foundation for Credit Counseling
  801 Roeder Road, Suite 900
  Silver Spring, MD 20910
  (301) 589-5600
  www.nfcc.org

Second Mortgages

I have to admit that second mortgages scare me. Too often, I have seen new parents who are homeowners take out home equity lines of credit or another home loan to pay unsecured debt and then get into far worse trouble. The benefit is, of course, that the interest rates are usually extremely favorable when compared to those of a credit card, especially if you've made late payments in the past, and you do get a tax break on that interest.

However, keep in mind that you're switching unsecured debt for secured debt! If you can't make your payments on the new home loan, you put your property in jeopardy. Is this the home where you're raising your child? Is this the home that you want her to grow up in and remember as the childhood home? Be careful.

A second mortgage *can* be a good option, but know beyond a shadow of a doubt that you can meet the new loan obligation. Weigh the low-rate, tax-deductible interest and smaller monthly payments against whatever closing costs you are charged as well as the ultimate price of the debt. Extending a credit card balance by many years, even with a better interest rate, will greatly increase the total debt payout.

Retirement Plan Loans

The final option I'll cover is borrowing from your tax-deferred retirement account. If you have saved up some cash in a 401(k), 403(b), or 457, you may be able to borrow some (up to half of your vested balance, with a $50,000 limit) of what you have accumulated. The interest rates are usually less than for a credit card, typically the prime lending rate plus a couple of percentage points. The loans are easy to get, too, with no credit check and minimal paperwork. You typically have five years to repay the loan.

There are downsides to these loans, of course: if you leave your job, whether voluntarily or you get fired, you have to pay it back almost immediately. If you can't, the IRS will consider the balance a "deemed distribution," and you'll be taxed on the earnings. Furthermore, if you're younger than age 59.5, you'll also be penalized 10 percent for an early withdrawal. Plan loans can work out to your advantage, but remember, this is your retirement money. It is not to be frittered away.

WHAT TO AVOID AT ALL COSTS

This chapter would not be complete without addressing some of the debt instruments that I consider the worst of the worst. If you are a new parent in financial trouble, one of your first thoughts for solving it may be to borrow more. This just makes no sense at all, and yet it is precisely what many people do. Part of the problem is the way some loan and credit products are marketed, as if another loan is the answer. There are a few places and loan options that I strongly recommend virtually everyone avoid.

Payday Loans

There are very few positive things to say about payday loans. Okay, as a one-off, super rare occurrence, they aren't completely bad. If used more than that, though, they can become a real nightmare. Although these deferred deposit debt products are common in low-income neighborhoods, thus catering to those who can least afford to pay the obscenely high finance fees, people from virtually all social strata and income levels use them.

This is how they work. You write a personal check, payable to the lender, for the amount you want to borrow plus a fee, which is typically 10 to 25 percent of the amount borrowed. The lender holds the check until your next payday, at which time you redeem the check by paying the amount you borrowed. If you don't have enough money to cover the check, you may roll it over for another term, but another fee is added to the balance. Many people get caught up in a payday loan trap because it can be difficult to repay the entire loan when their payday arrives; doing so would leave them with little or no money for current living expenses. Some payday lenders may even require you to sign an "Assignment of Salary and Wages." This allows them to go directly to your employer and deduct the amount you borrowed straight from your paycheck.

High Interest Unsecured Loans

You may have heard the commercials: "No credit, bad credit? No problem! We can have $10,000 in your account overnight!" With a new baby, it can be mighty tempting to call the number provided to get your hands on some extra spending money. However, in almost all cases, these loan

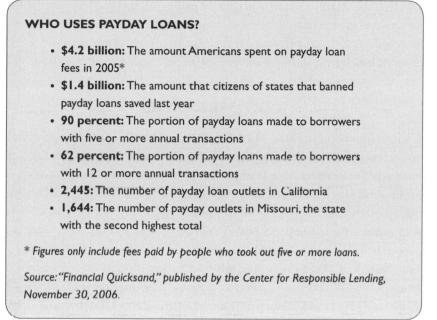

WHO USES PAYDAY LOANS?

- **$4.2 billion:** The amount Americans spent on payday loan fees in 2005*
- **$1.4 billion:** The amount that citizens of states that banned payday loans saved last year
- **90 percent:** The portion of payday loans made to borrowers with five or more annual transactions
- **62 percent:** The portion of payday loans made to borrowers with 12 or more annual transactions
- **2,445:** The number of payday loan outlets in California
- **1,644:** The number of payday outlets in Missouri, the state with the second highest total

Figures only include fees paid by people who took out five or more loans.

Source: "Financial Quicksand," published by the Center for Responsible Lending, November 30, 2006.

products should be avoided. With interest rates in the 45 to 90 percent range, they do not work in anyone's favor but the lender's.

BANKRUPTCY: THE FINAL CHAPTER?

I just spent a lot of time talking about repaying your debts for the greater good of your family, but there are other options for dealing with debt that you may want to consider. Before I get into them, remember this: your main priority is to take care of your family the best way you can, not just right now but over the long term as well. That can mean making some very hard decisions and taking actions that you may not like but that can really help in making your quest for a sound future a reality.

Sometimes, bankruptcy is the best way to get relief from overwhelming debt. If you have no way of repaying your balances because your income is simply insufficient, discharging your debt is a way to start over. Not everyone can file for Chapter 7 bankruptcy; you have to prove need and go through required counseling. If you are able to do it, you'll walk away from unsecured debts—credit card, medical bills, collection accounts, and the like. It will remain a matter of public record for ten years. That means that if you have a newborn now, he will be entering fifth grade by the time it drops off your credit reports. Bankruptcy is never to be entered into lightly and without exploring all other alternatives first.

GOOD DEBT EXISTS!

It's important to note that not all debt is equal, and this chapter is not a condemnation of all loans. In fact, the ability to borrow and finance your goals is intrinsic to a healthy financial picture. Few among us can purchase a home outright, so a mortgage of hundreds of thousands of dollars often makes sense and has a tax benefit, too. You may want to start your own business and need capital to get it off the ground. As long as the project is viable, go forth and borrow. What about financing an education? I can't think of a better reason to take out a loan. If the skills you learn will ultimately make you into a great candidate for a better paying job, fill out those loan papers today. Keep in mind, though, that good debt can quickly turn sour if you take out too much or just can't make your payments. Again, I can't stress enough being conservative with what you borrow.

DEBT-FREE NOW? KEEP IT THAT WAY.

Even if you don't owe a penny at this moment, impending and new parenthood just may be the event that could change all that. This is a pivotal moment in your life, but be careful—a lot of great intentions can go wayward. You, too, can be caught in the debt trap if your financial circumstances change drastically. The expenses involved in raising a new baby can do just that.

Again, go back to your cash-flow worksheet. At this point in your life, how much do you have left for new baby expenses? Let's say your baby fits within the national average and costs around $10,000 to raise during the first year of her life. Break that figure down to a monthly expense, and it's somewhere around $830. Do you have that amount of money in extra income just sitting around, after setting aside cash for your emergency savings account, retirement fund, and other investments and savings? If you do, terrific; you won't need those credit cards then—off to Babies "R" Us with you. If you don't, you may be tempted to begin charging for all those extra expenses. Resist. Your family's financial security matters so much more than all of those things, doesn't it?

Credit cards and other consumer debt instruments are neither friends nor foes; they are just tools. However, just as you can whack your thumb with a hammer while building your new baby's bookshelf, putting your hand out of commission for a while, so too can you damage your finances by misusing your credit tools from overcharging and underplanning. More people than ever are borrowing their way into financial instability, but you can be a leader in debt defiance. Have confidence in your strength and ability to repay whatever debt you may have, and prepare for the future so you aren't tempted to borrow your way out of problems.

CHAPTER SUMMARY

- Always spend within your means—don't rely on credit cards to get you through the hard times or pay for what you can't afford
- Think of credit cards as a short-term loan. Repay the balance in full after a few months at the most.
- Become informed and use the right type of credit for your financial situation and needs.
- Monitor your credit reports and build a positive credit history and score.
- Avoid being overly optimistic or pessimistic about debt and debt repayment.
- Use credit to your family's advantage by getting and using the right cards for your lifestyle and needs.
- If you have high-interest consumer debt now, make repaying it a top priority:
  - Suspend charging.
  - Figure out how much you can apply toward the debt by reviewing your cash flow.
  - Get assistance if you need it.
- Remain debt-free by prioritizing what you need and saving for emergencies and goals.

Chapter 4

Employee Benefits

Know Your Options

I F YOU PLAN ON returning to work after your baby is born, then you probably have a few questions regarding your job. Exploring all of the employee benefits that may be available to you should be an essential part of your planning for baby's arrival. By preparing in advance and knowing what options are available, you'll be in a much better position to plan effectively.

EMPLOYMENT ISSUES

Dealing with employment issues and new parenthood isn't always easy. Countless parents feel quite a bit of anxiety regarding pregnancy and parental leave. It is common for expecting parents to worry about whether or not they'll be able to hold onto their jobs once their baby arrives, and they are hesitant to explore what options might be available to them out of fear of jeopardizing their position. Because of this, every new mother and father who works outside the home should be aware of their legal rights concerning employment, pregnancy, and parenthood. Many workers are unaware of the options that are available and consequently never take advantage of the support and tax advantages their employers might provide.

Too many new parents take the worst approach possible: they play the entire process of dealing with work and income issues by ear. By crossing your fingers and hoping it will all work out somehow or giving in to the fear that if you ask for time off after your child is born, you'll lose your job, you can miss out on valuable emotional and financial security—and hurt your ability to plan effectively. Feeling financially vulnerable is often a by-product simply of not knowing. Therefore, while the subject of employee benefits may not always be the easiest to address, getting a handle on it will put you in a position of real power, always the best place to be.

The Income Impact

If your income is going to be reduced when your baby arrives, you need to know by exactly how much and for precisely how long. There really is no such a thing as universal "maternity leave" in the United States. The amount of time you can take off before returning to work depends on quite a few factors, such as the state you live in, your company's policy, and the number of people employed by your company.

As mentioned, you should find out your company's policy concerning pre- and postpartum employees as soon as possible. Some companies are known for their liberal attitude toward parenthood, while others are more "business as usual" and don't give new mothers and fathers much of a break. If you have an employee handbook, now is the time to crack it open. If you don't, ask your human resources professional or even another coworker who has been through the experience for information and advice.

Having the "Time-Off Talk" With Your Employer

Some of your most important and pressing concerns are likely about time: How long *should* you take off? How much time would you *like* to take off? How much time are you *entitled* to take off? Finally, how much are you financially *able* to take off?

WORKING PARENTS—HOW THE UNITED STATES COMPARES WITH THE REST OF THE WORLD

As parents, do we have it better or worse than the rest of the world? You may be surprised at how we fare:

- Out of 173 countries surveyed, 168 guarantee paid maternal leave, and 98 countries offer 14 or more weeks of paid leave. The United States provides no paid leave for mothers. Lesotho, Liberia, Swaziland, and Papua New Guinea are the only other countries surveyed that do not guarantee paid leave to mothers.
- Sixty-five countries grant fathers either paid paternity leave or paid parental leave, with 31 of these countries offering 14 or more weeks of paid leave. The United States guarantees fathers neither paid paternity nor paid parental leave.
- At least 107 countries protect working women's right to breast-feed, and the breaks are paid in at least 73 of these countries. The United States does not guarantee the right to breast-feed, even though breast-feeding is demonstrated to reduce infant mortality 150 to 500 percent.
- At least 145 countries provide paid sick days for short- or long-term illnesses, with 127 providing a week or more annually. The United States provides unpaid leave only for serious illnesses through the Family and Medical Leave Act, which does not cover all workers, and has no federal law providing for paid sick days.

Source: The 2007 Work, Family, and Equity Index: How Does the U.S. Measure Up?, 2004 Harvard study by IHSP Director Dr. Jody Heymann.

Unfortunately, many new parents end up going back to work far sooner than they would prefer. According to a 2006 study conducted by the School of Public Health at the University of Minnesota, nearly one in six employed mothers returns to her job within the *first month* after delivery—not by choice but out of economic need.

Are you planning on going back to work at some point after your new baby arrives? Then the last thing you want is to create less-than-friendly circumstances. That's why it's important to inform your employer regarding your time-off plans and negotiate a mutually beneficial schedule with your boss in a positive way. Be candid, patient, open, and flexible when you bring the up the subject but stick to your guns. This is your life, not anyone else's, and your efforts should serve the needs of your growing family.

Once you have a good idea of how you're going to approach this issue, determine precisely whom you need to initiate this discussion with. Should you approach your immediate supervisor or your employer's human resources professional (if there is one)? The latter is usually the preferred method, simply because that person is normally the one who is most informed regarding company policy and is supposed to be a neutral party.

Your current relationship with your employer will likely factor into how you choose to address this subject. However, even if you and your immediate supervisor are on friendly terms, it is best to keep this discussion on a completely professional level. Before you begin your talk, find out what your maternity/paternity leave options are. Again, if you have an employee handbook, read it. It should spell things out in detail. Knowing your rights can go a long way when broaching this topic with your employer.

As far as when to start this talk, your employer will likely appreciate knowing your plans as early as possible, which can certainly work in your favor. You may be eager to set up your finances right away and want to march straight over to human resources the day you find out about the pregnancy. However, many people choose to wait until the risk of miscarriage goes down a bit, usually after the first trimester. The choice is yours.

Don't leave it up to your employer to come up with scheduling ideas for you. Before you speak with anyone at your company, come up with ideas that you think might work and prioritize them according to what appeals to you most. It's up to you to determine how much time off you want and need. If you don't want to return as a full-time employee, determine what arrangement will work best for you and your family. Determine how much paid leave you have available. Research your state and federal family leave and disability laws. If you're considering unpaid leave, think about how long you can reasonably afford to go without

STAY IN TOUCH!

Although staying in touch with your employer and addressing work concerns may not be at the top of your list while you're out on leave with your new baby, it can often benefit you, especially if you are a top-level employee. According to a 2005 study conducted by The Ladders.com, a website for workers earning annual salaries of $100,000 or more, many executive parents risk workplace resentment for taking time off to raise their kids:

- Asked to describe their feelings about top-level employees returning to work after an extended parental leave, almost half of over 1,000 executives polled said they were "resented for taking time off."
- About a quarter felt that those who took a multiyear hiatus were "too far removed from the action to be effective."
- When asked what they would do if they had children and money was no object, 53 percent said they would stay on the job with a reduced workload. Another 9 percent said they would continue working full-time. In contrast, 39 percent said they would be stay-at-home parents.
- Although the average maternity leave in today's workplace is 9 weeks, of those polled, 44 percent said they received 6 weeks leave, 27 percent got 12 weeks, and 17 percent got 8 weeks. Only 6 percent received 16 weeks or more.

What's the bottom line? Try not to get too far removed from what's going on at the office. If possible, send the occasional email, read over important documents (especially if there is anything "new" going on—you will want to know about it), and even consider meeting up with a colleague during your time off if you can manage it.

your salary. Remember, you have until the end of your leave to decide whether you'll come back full-time, part-time, or not at all.

When talking with your employer, be calm yet confident and do your best to help your employer work with you towards creating a schedule that meets both your needs. Even if you don't think all of your propositions are viable, offer solutions rather than problems by having some ideas for how your work can be handled while you're away. Again, do your best to be as honest as possible. Don't say you're going to come back if you have no intention of doing so. Someday you may want to re-enter the workforce, and you never want to burn bridges. You have the right to keep your options open.

If you are a valued employee, most likely your employer will do whatever it can to keep you, so avoid procrastinating and start planning for your talk. You shouldn't wait to have this discussion until after you've used up all of your sick days because of morning sickness. There are lots of other issues going on in your life right now, and you'll be glad once this is taken care of.

Vacation/Personal/Sick Days

In preparation for baby's arrival, many women begin to accumulate as many vacation, personal, and sick days as possible before they go out on maternity leave or to use after the birth or adoption of their baby. In general, hoarding these hours is a great idea, although if you are too ill to work, don't push yourself just for the sake of saving sick days. You'll be able to add all of those days to the time you take off while you are being paid short-term disability benefits, thus extending your time off from work to be with your baby. In most cases, you do have to use all of those hours before any insurance benefit kicks in.

Short-Term Disability

Short-term disability (SDI) plans are insurance policies that provide you with cash benefits if you cannot work for a relatively short period of time due to injury, illness, pregnancy, and post-pregnancy recovery. In other words, if you have a short-term disability, you'll be getting at least some income during the time you take off before the birth of your baby and/or afterwards. Do note, however, that these benefits are only meant to *supplement* what you have saved. They are very rarely the same amount as your monthly paycheck. Your mortgage and other household expenses aren't going to be similarly reduced during the time you take off, so planning for this reduction by saving for the shortfall, however temporary, is crucial.

How much you get from your short-term disability policy depends on different factors. If you have it through your employer or if you purchased it yourself, the insurance provider will generally pay you between 50 and 100 percent of your current salary for a set number of weeks (with a cap), depending on how many years you've worked for the company and the specific details of your individual policy. In general, six weeks is the standard amount of time covered for pregnancy, although some policies allow more time if you've had complications or a cesarean delivery. Many short-term disability plans provide other sorts of coverage, such as for bed rest prior to birth, so research the specifics of your particular plan.

State-sponsored plans are usually a little different. They typically cover one-half to two-thirds of your salary. The coverage time frame for pregnancy is usually 4 to 6 weeks, but in some circumstances, such as when there exists a medical need, it can last up to 12 weeks. As of this writing, only California, Hawaii, Rhode Island, New Jersey, and New York have state-sponsored plans. If you live in one of those states, the mandatory contributions come right out of your paycheck, without your ever having to sign up. Your employer may be so kind as to pick up the tab for this, though if you pay, then you get to deduct the contributions on your federal income taxes.

When both your state and your company offer short-term disability coverage, in many cases, you have to use the full state benefit before your employer's coverage makes up for any additional time off, if you take it. In other words, if you are entitled to both plans, you won't get twice the coverage but rather the minimum from the most generous plan.

Be aware that most short-term disability plans require that you be out of work for up to one week before you can start to collect disability benefits, and you'll probably have to use up your accrued sick days or vacation days before your disability benefits kick in. Therefore, if you have no accumulated paid days off, you'll probably have a week of no pay at all. That can be a very big ouch!

As far as taxes go, whether or not you have to pay them depends on who covers the insurance premiums:

- State SDI distributions are generally not subject to federal or state income taxes.
- If you pay for the disability insurance premiums yourself, the benefits you receive are tax-free.

- Whatever portion of your salary that you receive from your employer's coverage is taxable. No income taxes will be taken out of your checks, so you'll end up owing the money in April.

Let's take a look at how much you might receive in benefits. Here's an example. Let's say you have accumulated 80 hours of vacation time, which is 10 days of full pay. You plan on taking three full months off to be with your baby before going back to

> **TIME-OFF TIP**
>
> Some employers allow other staff members to donate or gift their unused hours. If your work friends are planning on throwing you a goodbye party or baby shower, do look into this!

work on a part-time schedule. After speaking with your human resources department and learning more about your short-term disability benefits, you find that you're going to receive 60 percent of your salary for a total of six weeks. You normally take home $2,100 per month, so 60 percent is $1,260, paid out on a weekly basis of $315 for those six weeks.

Desired time frame	= 3 months/12 weeks
10 days at 100% pay	= $1,050
6 weeks at 60% pay	= $1,890
Total	= $2,940
Normal income for 3 months	= $6,300
Total Difference	= $3,360 ($6,300 − $2,940 = $3,360)

In essence, by taking time off to be with your baby, you will be seeing a decrease in income. In this example, the amount that was "lost" was $3,360 over three months. For most families, this is a considerable amount of money. Yours could be more or less of course, depending upon your specific situation. Determine precisely what your loss might be, so it doesn't come as a nasty surprise.

After computing the amount of money you may lose by not working, consider ways that you can make up the difference. Perhaps you are still working right now and can generate more sick or vacation hours by working as much as you can before delivery. Maybe your partner can increase work hours during this time and amplify savings. Another option to lessen the financial hit is to find areas in your budget where you can cut down temporarily and save the difference. In short, consider all options, brainstorm ideas, and get creative. Your family's financial well-being is paramount, so do whatever you can do to ensure it.

Unpaid Disability Leave

If you are not ready, willing, or able to return to your job after your short-term disability coverage ends, you may be able to take unpaid disability leave under the Family and Medical Leave Act. Whether you are a public or private sector employee, if you've been on the job for at least one year and have worked at least 1,250 hours, you are entitled to take up to 12 weeks of unpaid leave in any 12-month period for the birth or adoption of a child and for other reasons as well, such as if you, your child, your spouse, or your parent is seriously ill.

California, Connecticut, District of Columbia, Louisiana, Oregon, Puerto Rico, Rhode Island, and Tennessee offer even longer leaves of absence. In most states, this law does not cover companies with fewer than 50 employees. The current exceptions are Oregon (25 or more), District of Columbia (20 or more), Maine (15 or more), and Vermont (10 or more). During this time, you won't get a paycheck or disability payments, but your employer will be legally required to reserve your job for you until you return.

To learn how unpaid disability can work for you, talk with your employer. For planning purposes, the sooner you have this discussion, the better. Federal guidelines require you to request this leave at least 30 days before you plan on leaving your job, but as a courtesy you may want to give your employer a bit more notice. After all, if you're planning to go back to work, you want to keep good relations with your boss and company. A little extra notice about your intentions can really work in your favor.

What follows are some of the key points of the Family and Medical Leave Act (FMLA):

- It doesn't matter if you are male or female.
- You can take your leave intermittently, though it is subject to employer approval.

- If both you and your spouse work for the same employer, the total amount of leave that you may take is limited to 12 weeks if you are taking leave for the birth or adoption of a child or to care for a sick parent.
- You may elect or your employer may require you to substitute categories of paid leave, such as accrued time off or vacation time, for any part of the 12-week period.
- Your employer must maintain any pre-existing health insurance for the duration of the leave at the same level and under the same conditions that coverage was provided before you left. However, employers can ask you to cover your share of the premiums. Employers are not required to continue such benefits as life and disability insurance, though they can't require you to requalify for them.
- Upon your return, your employer must provide you with your original or an equivalent position with the same benefits, pay, and all other terms and conditions of employment.
- You may need to provide your employer with certification from a health care provider to support a claim for leave.
- You are required to provide at least 30 days' advance notice before taking your leave.
- If you are among the highest-paid 10 percent of salaried employees, you may be denied job restoration.
- FMLA does not supersede any state or local law, collective bargaining agreement, or employment benefit plan that provides greater employee family leave rights, nor does it diminish the capacity to adopt more generous family leave policies.

Essentially, if you are worried that your boss can dictate when you are able to stop working and go out on leave to care for your baby, relax—no one can make that decision but you. If you want to leave your job during your pregnancy to prepare for your baby's arrival, you can do that. Financially speaking, it is best to be prudent with your time because the

---

HOW DOES YOUR STATE STACK UP?

In the 2005 *Expecting Better: A State-by-State Analysis of Parental Leave Policies*, the National Partnership for Women and Families rated each state's laws concerning worker's rights and taking time off to care for children. Become familiar with your own state's policy (Figure 4.1) so you know what to expect with respect to your job.

---

sooner you start your leave, the sooner it will run out after your baby's born. For more information about your legal rights concerning employment, pregnancy, and caring for your young child, contact

- U.S. Department of Labor
  Wage and Hour Division
  200 Constitution Avenue NW
  Washington, DC 20210
  866-487-9243
  www.dol.gov

- Families and Work Institute
  267 Fifth Avenue, 2nd Floor
  New York, NY 10016
  (212) 465-2044
  www.familiesandwork.org

If you have any questions or would like additional information, contact

- National Partnership for Women & Families
  1875 Connecticut Avenue NW, Suite 710
  Washington, DC 20009
  (202) 986-2600
  www.nationalpartnership.org

Figure 4.1 *State-by-State Workers Rights Comparison Chart*

	Paid Leave for Private Sector Employees			
	Family Leave Benefits	Medical/ Maternity Leave Benefits	Flexible Sick Days	At-Home Infant Care Benefits
Alabama				
Alaska				
Arizona				
Arkansas				
California	▨	▨	*	
Colorado				
Connecticut			▨	
Delaware				
Florida				
Georgia				
Hawaii		▨	▨	
Idaho				
Illinois				
Indiana				
Iowa				
Kansas				
Kentucky				
Louisiana				
Maine				
Maryland				
Massachusetts				
Michigan				
Minnesota				▨
Mississippi				
Missouri				
Montana				**
Nebraska				
Nevada				
New Hampshire				
New Jersey		▨		

▨ = Existing state worker benefit.

* California has a flexible sick leave law that entitles all workers who have access to sick leave to use it to care for a seriously ill spouse or partner temporarily disabled due to pregnancy or recovery from childbirth but not to care for a newborn. See California Labor Code 233.

** To date, Montana's at-home infant care benefits program remains unfunded.

Extension of Unpaid Job-Protected FMLA			State Laws	State Employees	
Expanded Job-Protected Family Leave	Expanded Job-Protected Medical/ Maternity Leave	Extended Length of Job-Protected Family and Medical Leave	State Family Medical Leave Laws	Paid Family and Medical Leave Benefits	Extended Length of Job-Protected Family and Medical Leave
					░
	░	░	░		░
	░	░	░		░
					░
	░		░	░	░
				░	
					░
	░				
					░
	░		░		
░	░		░		
░	░				░
					░
░			░		░
	░				
	░				░
		░	░	░	░

(continued)

Figure 4.1 *State-by-State Workers Rights Comparison Chart (continued)*

	Paid Leave for Private Sector Employees			
	Family Leave Benefits	Medical/ Maternity Leave Benefits	Flexible Sick Days	At-Home Infant Care Benefits
New Mexico				▓
New York		▓		
North Carolina				
North Dakota				
Ohio				
Oklahoma				
Oregon				
Pennsylvania				
Rhode Island		▓		
South Carolina				
South Dakota				
Tennessee				
Texas				
Utah				
Vermont				
Virginia				
Washington			▓	
West Virginia				
Wisconsin			▓	
Wyoming				
District of Columbia				
Federal employees				

▓ = *Existing state worker benefit.*

Additional information on the rights of parents in the workforce can be found on the website of Moms Rising, a nonprofit organization that is working toward passing more family-friendly legislation. Go to *www.momsrising.org* to learn more.

More Employee Benefits

When was the last time you checked up on what benefits your employer offers? If it's been a while, you should certainly do a little research—you

Extension of Unpaid Job-Protected FMLA			State Laws	State Employees	
Expanded Job-Protected Family Leave	Expanded Job-Protected Medical/ Maternity Leave	Extended Length of Job-Protected Family and Medical Leave	State Family Medical Leave Laws	Paid Family and Medical Leave Benefits	Extended Length of Job-Protected Family and Medical Leave

may have some options that can help save money, both while you're pregnant as well as long into your family's future. It's remarkable how many people have great benefits and never take advantage.

Flexible Spending Accounts. A flexible spending account (FSA) is a tax-advantaged financial account wherein you can set aside a portion of your pretax earnings to pay for qualified expenses. If you have the opportunity to use one, do so, because you can save a lot of money this way.

You'll be able to set aside cash for medical and child care expenses. All you need to do is determine an amount that you want to have deducted from your paycheck to be deposited into an FSA. As with many employee benefits, you can sign up for these accounts during your annual open enrollment period. The three most common types are dependant care FSAs, medical expense FSAs, and transportation savings accounts.

As a new parent, you are going to want to save money everywhere you can. Child care expenses can be astronomical, so if you have the opportunity to use an FSA to set aside cash to cover at least some of those expenses, don't waste it. With a FSA, you can set aside a maximum of $5,000 in pretax earnings per year ($2,500 per year if married and filing separately) for qualified dependant care costs. Any child under age 13 is eligible, as long as he is living with you and you can claim him as a dependent. All it takes to set up a dependant care FSA is to fill out a simple form that your employer can provide.

How much money can you save? Assuming an annual income of $40,000, a 15 percent tax bracket, and estimated dependent care expenses of $5,000, your tax savings will be approximately $472 annually. Figure 4.2 outlines the potential savings.

Just by setting aside money in a dependant care FSA, you can save almost $500. I'm sure that when your baby arrives, you can think of a few terrific ways to spend that kind of money.

Medical Expense FSA. Another type of FSA that may be available to you is the medical expense FSA (also called a health care FSA). This is a way to pay for medical expenses that your insurance does not cover. Because medical expenses are often a significant slice of a new family's budget, setting aside pretax dollars for deductibles, copayments, dental and vision expenses, and even some over-the-counter medicines can really save you money. The amount you can set aside in these accounts varies, because individual employers set the cap.

To know how much to set aside, estimate the amount you think you may spend for the year. How much could that potentially be? Well, many new families shell out several hundred dollars in copayments for their newborn in the first year alone. If you were to take your baby in to see the pediatrician 12 times and the copayment is $20, you would be spending

Figure 4.2 *Dependant Care FSA Chart*

DEPENDANT CARE FSA CHART			
	With FSA	**Without FSA**	**FSA Savings**
Annual Income:	$40,000	$40,000	
Estimated Dependent Care Pretax Contributions:	$5,000	$0	
Taxable Income:	$35,000	$40,000	
Estimated Federal Withholding:	$4,713	$5,463	
Estimated FICA:	$2,678	$3,060	
Dependent Care Expenses (without FSA):	$0	$5,000	
Tax Credit for Dependent Care:	$0	$660	
Net Pay:	**$27,609**	**$27,137**	**$472**

Filing Status: Head of Household with one dependent. These projections are only estimates of 2006 tax information. Table from Aetna www.aetna.com/fsa/understanding/dependent/dependent_care.html#s1

$240—and that's just for baby. As a postpartum mother, you'll be having quite a few checkups as well. Start there and work your way up. These accounts are prefunded, meaning that after you figure out how much you'd like to use for the year and complete the paperwork, that sum is available to you from the start.

While there is no "use it or lose it" rule, so any money you don't spend simply rolls over for the next year, there are spending limits. Each year these restrictions change. Check with the IRS for account limit information.

Transportation Savings Accounts. Your employer may also offer transportation savings accounts, which allow you to direct a portion of your pretax income into a special account that you use for qualified work-related transportation expenses. These may include employment-related parking expenses, public transportation costs, and vanpooling expenses. Anywhere you can whittle those taxes down is great. If you have those costs, it just makes sense to get the tax break—it's more money in your family's combined pocket.

Employee Assistance Plans. Many companies contract with employee assistance plans (EAPs) as an added benefit. If your company offers this to you, be sure to see what it provides for expecting parents and new families. There may very well be programs that can make your life a whole lot easier. For example, your EAP may offer special pregnancy assistance services, where you may receive a free pregnancy education kit with a pregnancy calendar, and specialized care management, where a team of obstetrical nurses work with your physician to coordinate expert care.

If you need pre- or postpartum counseling services, your EAP can step in and help you find a doctor or counselor. If you are seeking child care in your area, your EAP may work with you to find someone who fits exactly what you need in terms of location, cost, and other factors. This can be really helpful when you haven't got a clue where to begin finding child care that you are comfortable with.

Many employers provide EAP services because they want happy, healthy employees. Take advantage of what your employer has to offer, including no-cost services. As a new parent, you can probably use all the "free" you can get.

Pregnancy Rights. Talk with your employer about your pregnancy-related plans and situation. To give you a bit of emotional strength, know how the law protects you. The Pregnancy Discrimination Act is actually an amendment to the Civil Rights Act of 1964. It stipulates that discrimination on the basis of pregnancy, childbirth, or related medical conditions constitutes unlawful sex discrimination. Women affected by pregnancy or related conditions must be treated in the same manner as other applicants or employees with similar abilities or limitations.

- **Hiring.** An employer cannot refuse to hire a woman because she is pregnant, as long as she is able to perform the major functions of the job. An employer cannot refuse to hire a woman because of its prejudices against pregnant workers or the prejudices of coworkers, clients, or customers.
- **Pregnancy and Maternity Leave.** An employer may not single out a worker's pregnancy-related condition as a condition for determining her ability to work. However,

an employer may use any procedure used to screen other employees' ability to work. For example, if an employer requires its employees to submit a doctor's statement concerning their inability to work before granting leave or paying sick benefits, the employer may require pregnant employees to submit such statements.

- **Fair Treatment.** If an employee is temporarily unable to perform her job due to pregnancy, the employer must treat her the same as any other temporarily disabled employee; for example, by providing modified tasks, alternative assignments, disability leave, or leave without pay. Pregnant employees must be permitted to work as long as they are able to perform their jobs. If an employee has been absent from work as a result of a pregnancy-related condition and recovers, her employer may not require her to remain on leave until the baby's birth. An employer may not have a rule that prohibits an employee from returning to work for a predetermined length of time after childbirth. Employers must hold open a job for a pregnancy-related absence the same length of time jobs are held open for employees on sick or disability leave.

- **Health Insurance.** Any health insurance provided by an employer must cover expenses for pregnancy-related conditions on the same basis as costs for other medical conditions. Health insurance for expenses arising from abortion is not required, except where the life of the mother is endangered. Pregnancy-related expenses should be reimbursed exactly like those incurred for other medical conditions, whether payment is on a fixed basis or a percentage of reasonable and customary charge basis. The amounts payable by the insurance provider can be limited only to the same extent as costs for other conditions. No additional, increased, or larger deductible can be imposed. Employers must provide the same level of health benefits for spouses of male employees as they do for spouses of female employees.

- **Fringe Benefits.** Pregnancy-related benefits cannot be limited to married employees. In an all-female workforce or job classification, benefits must be provided for pregnancy-related conditions if benefits are provided for other medical conditions. If an employer provides any benefits to workers on leave, the employer must provide the same benefits for those on leave for pregnancy-related conditions. Employees with pregnancy-related disabilities must be treated the same as other temporarily disabled employees for accrual and crediting of seniority, vacation calculation, pay increases, and temporary disability benefits.

Source: The U.S. Equal Employment Opportunity Commission.

When addressing the issue of employee benefits, it's never a good idea to plan your financial future without knowing all of your options, rights, and benefits. Once you become informed, you'll be far more prepared to make the best economic decisions for your growing family.

CHAPTER SUMMARY

- Put yourself in a position of power by knowing your rights and benefits as an employee.
- Communicate with your employer about your desired plans effectively:
  - o Formulate a plan.
  - o Speak with the right people.
  - o Choose the right time.
  - o Be honest, flexible, and confident.
  - o Work towards developing a plan that meets the needs of both your employer and your family.
- Learn more about your state's policy concerning work and parenting; you may have extra protection coming to you.
- Figure out how much time you want off and how much (if any) disability and other benefits will pay.

- Begin to accumulate your vacation/personal/sick days early and use them prudently.
- Understand how short-term disability can work for you.
- If you think you'll be taking unpaid disability leave, know your rights under the Family and Medical Leave Act.
- Understand and utilize all of the employee benefits that make sense for you:
  - o Reduce your taxes through flexible spending accounts.
  - o Utilize your company's employee assistance plan if one is available to you.
- Learn how the Pregnancy Discrimination Act protects your rights while you are expecting.

Chapter 5

Bringing Baby Home Healthy

Fertility, Adoption, Health Care, and Parenting Education Expenses

L ONG BEFORE YOU ATTEMPT to start a family, you may wonder *why* children, babies in particular, should have such a major impact on your finances. How can someone so tiny cost so much? For some, the answer to that question begins with the cost of becoming a parent in the first place. According to 2002 information provided by the National Center for Health Statistics of the Centers for Disease Control and Prevention, about 12 percent of women in the United States age 15–44 had difficulty getting pregnant or carrying a baby to term. You may be among the millions of people who go through fertility treatments in an effort to overcome this, procedures that are often outrageously pricey. Maybe you will become, or already are, an adoptive parent, also a process that is not inexpensive. However, you can prepare for it—as you can for all new parenting costs—if you know what to expect beforehand.

In addition, all new and expecting parents must plan for both expected and unforeseen health care costs. Financial and physical health are closely linked and should be managed with utmost care. Charges for labor and delivery can be substantial, whether you have insurance or not. Therefore, preparing for these costs as early as possible is your best strategy.

As you make arrangements for the birth of your child, you'll notice that there are many options and factors to consider, each with its own price tag, benefits, and potential drawbacks. Remember to make your choices based upon your medical and financial needs. For instance, you may choose to pay extra for a private room in a hospital for your labor or hire a professional childbirth advocate to provide support and guidance. Then there are the increased insurance copayments for pregnant women and newborns, which can quickly add up and throw a monthly budget off if you're not planning for them. Perhaps your child has or will have health problems, which may result in increased trips to the doctor or hospital, expensive treatments and medications, and having to take time off of work, thus decreasing your income.

The number of financial decisions you need to make when it comes to bringing your baby home can be daunting. Furthermore, because they all seem important, prioritization can be tough. You want to do the right thing, but discerning exactly what this means can be hard. Perhaps you'd like to take parenting classes or bank something called "cord blood." Maybe you want a preview of your baby *in utero;* all of these costly extras can pile up. To plan properly and not get sideswiped by any of these costs, you've got to know what they could be and, whenever possible, factor them into your budget responsibly and realistically.

FERTILITY EXPENSES

Okay, let's start at the beginning: getting pregnant. If you are in the process of trying to conceive by way of fertility treatments, you already know that there are fees involved. Depending on the method you choose or need, the cost of becoming pregnant can be considerable.

Many of these medical procedures are not even partially covered by health insurance, although the state you live in may offer some relief. As of this writing, Arkansas, California, Connecticut, Hawaii, Illinois, Maryland, Massachusetts, Montana, New Jersey, New York, Ohio, Rhode Island, Texas, and West Virginia do require insurers to cover the cost of fertility diagnosis as well as to pay for the cost of some treatments. Contact your state's insurance commissioner's office for detailed and current information about your state's regulations: *www.naic.org/state_web_map.htm*.

Most of the time, however, you'll be paying for the majority of the expenses out of your own pocket. Of course, you can charge much of it, and many do, but be aware that some financial institutions provide loans specifically for fertility treatments.

What follows is a broad overview of the cost of the most common types of fertility treatments that are currently available, beginning with the least expensive and working upward. Check with your individual health insurance policy for which procedures may be covered, as this can fluctuate. This is not meant to be taken as medical advice or an endorsement of any one method over another, but it will give you some round numbers from which to begin your financial planning. As previously stated, nothing is more frustrating when trying to plan than not having an idea about what something might cost. When you are considering any and all treatments, always consult with your doctor and other medical professionals first.

Acupuncture

For a growing number of women, acupuncture is the first step toward having a baby biologically because it is noninvasive and relatively affordable. Acupuncture is Chinese in origin and involves placing hair-sized needles into your skin. The idea is to stimulate specific energy points that are linked to your reproductive organs. The cost of acupuncture treatments is about $50–$100 per session, or about $1,000 for a 12-treatment program.

Ovulation Induction

In this procedure, medications (such as Clomid) are used to help induce ovulation. These fertility drugs can be used alone or with other therapies. The typical cost for this type of medication is $50 per treatment, and many women use it for between three to six menstrual cycles. However, this does not include the cost of doctor visits (your copayments may be nothing or upwards of $50 per visit) and other medical procedures that people who use this type of treatment also receive.

Intrauterine Insemination (IUI)

IUI is a fairly basic (not to be confused with inexpensive) method of fertility treatment. Essentially, it is sperm insemination. The cost of this therapy varies greatly depending on the amount of medication, ultrasounds, and other medical treatments that are needed, but the average is about $1,500–$2,000 per cycle. The number of cycles of treatment you need depends on how quickly you conceive, of course. Simple math gives us a figure of around $8,000–$10,000 for giving it a go six times, which many women do before conceiving with this method.

In Vitro Fertilization

Considerably less simple, and therefore more costly, is *in vitro* fertilization (IVF). This is where a woman typically, but not always, takes fertility medication to encourage her body to produce multiple eggs. The eggs are removed and inseminated. According to the American Society of Reproductive Medicine, the current average cost of IVF is $12,400 per treatment. There are no guarantees that it will work the first time around, so it isn't hard to imagine how costly this option can potentially become.

Egg Donors

Egg donors are used when a woman is unable to produce her own eggs or the eggs that she does produce are of low quality. This is often the case in older women or women who have experienced premature menopause. The donor eggs are then inseminated in the IVF process and placed inside the birth mother's uterus. Hold on to your hat (or bank account): getting pregnant via the egg donor process starts at around $20,000, not including the cost of various medications for one complete IVF cycle. Again, there are no guarantees, and many people go through the process more than once.

ADOPTION

Adoption is, of course, another option for having a child. As with the price to get pregnant, the cost to adopt ranges dramatically, depending on the type of adoption method you pursue. To understand each type, the potential costs involved, and general time lines, consider the informational chart developed by the North American Council on Adoptable Children (NACAC) (Figure 5.1).

Home Study Expenses

To begin the adoption process, you usually have to pay for something referred to as the home study process. Home study has multiple purposes. It is intended to educate and prepare you for adoption, to gather information about you so you will be matched with the "right" child, and to evaluate your fitness as a parent. The cost is usually somewhere between $1,000 and $3,000. If you adopt via foster care, the process is usually free of charge, though you may have to pay for other expenses like medical or psychological evaluations. If you adopt through an agency, the fee may be embedded in the cost.

Legal Fees

Most of the time, the adoption process includes attorneys' fees and court costs, which are the adoptive family's responsibility to pay. All domestic adoptions and some international adoptions must be finalized in a court in the United States. While some international adoptions are completed in the child's country of origin, many adoptive parents choose to do so in a U.S. court of law because it provides increased protection of their child's legal status. This may not come as a shock to you, but lawyers and other legal costs can be terribly expensive. Court document preparation can range from $500 to $2,000, while legal representation may range from $2,500 to $12,000 or more.

For more information about the rules, regulations, and processes of adoption, contact

- National Council For Adoption
  225 N. Washington Street
  Alexandria, VA 22314-2561
  (703) 299-6633
  www.adoptioncouncil.org
  ncfa@adoptioncouncil.org

Figure 5.1 *NACAC Chart of Adoption Types*

2006 NACAC CHART OF ADOPTION TYPES

Type of Adoption	Definition	Children Available	Approximate Cost	Who Can Adopt	How Long It Takes
Public Agency Adoption	An adoption directed and supervised by a state or local Department of Human Services, Social Services, Human Resources, Health and Welfare, Child and Family Services, etc.	Children with special needs (kids who are harder to place due to emotional or physical disorders, age, background, race, membership in a sibling group); rarely infants	From $0 to $2,000 (Depending on the state, up to $2,000 of "nonrecurring" adoption costs for eligible special-needs children may be reimbursed.)	Flexible eligibility requirements for adoptive parents; on a case-by-case basis, will consider single parents, parents over the age of 40, parents who have other children, parents with low incomes, etc.	Starts slowly, but for those who have an updated home study, placement can occur as soon as a few months after selecting a child.
Private Agency Adoption	An adoption directed and supervised by a privately funded, licensed adoption agency	Sometimes handle special-needs children; more commonly associated with younger children and infants.	$6,000 to $25,000; lower for special-needs children; some agencies have sliding fee scales.	Agencies may recruit parents based on race, religious affiliation, etc.; for infant adoptions, birth mother often chooses.	A few months to a few years (sometimes longer for infant adoption)
International Adoption	Process of adopting a child who is not a U.S. citizen, which may be accomplished privately through an attorney or through an international adoption agency	About 88 countries currently allow their children to be adopted by U.S. citizens (6 countries in Africa, 20 in Asia, 32 in Europe, and 30 in Latin America) ages range from infant to teens; health conditions vary.	$7,000 to $30,000 (varies by country; travel and travel-related expenses may be additional.)	Depends on agency and country requirements; some will accept single parents, most prospective parents are between 25 and 45 years old.	Six months to several years, depending on the child's age and health and the country's political climate
Independent Adoption (not legal in all states; also known as private adoption)	An adoption initiated by prospective adopters and completed with help from an attorney or adoption counselor	Generally infants	$5,000 to $40,000 (Includes cost of finding a birth mother, certain birth mother expenses, and attorney's fees.)	Birth mothers typically choose the adoptive parent. Preferences tend to run toward younger, affluent, married couples.	Variable; as long as it takes to find a birth mother who will see the process through to finalization

Source: North American Council on Adoptable Children (NACAC), 970 Raymond Avenue, Suite 106, St. Paul, MN 55114, (651) 644-3036, info@nacac.org

A FEW WORDS ABOUT PRICING PARENTHOOD

For many of us, the desire to become a parent is a powerful, nearly unstoppable drive. Because of this, it can be challenging to separate your emotions and break things down into simple financial terms. How can you put a price tag on a human life? However, addressing these concerns as realistically and methodically as possible is in your best interest. Clearly, major expenses are involved for most of the options, and if you don't have the cash, what are you going to do? Most likely, you'll either save or borrow for it. If having a baby is your goal, then go for it, but do your best to prepare. It is hardly uncommon to save tens of thousands for a down payment on a home, so why not for a child? It is a matter of priorities, and if yours is to become a parent, then take the financial steps necessary to make it happen.

PARENT EDUCATION

When I was pregnant with my daughter, one of the expenses I was most curious about was all the classes I was "expected" to take. Did I need to learn how to breathe during labor? Take lessons in diapering? What about sign language? I admit that in the end, I took none. Finding the time was just too difficult, and I wasn't sure I could justify the cost when I had both a mother and mother-in-law whom I could turn to for advice and support. However, I know that many pregnant women and new parents find some classes invaluable and absolutely worth the investment.

Some classes are held at hospitals and birthing centers (where you would think insurance would cover the tuition, but it often doesn't), while others are at off-site facilities. These tutorials range from free to outrageously expensive. In one popular San Francisco parent education center, classes are priced between $50 and $125 per session, and an astonishing number and array of programs are offered. Whether or not they are necessary is up to you, but if you're going to be paying for them, you may have to shell out some big bucks. As with most things, doing some research before you make a decision is your best strategy.

The following list is a summary of a roster of classes and workshops that are available at a typical parenting center:

- Musical play
- Infant and child CPR
- Newborn care
- Practical first aid
- Wills, trusts, and life insurance for new families
- Childbirth preparation
- Infant massage
- Preparing your dog for a new baby
- Breast-feeding
- Sign language for your baby
- Using your breast pump
- Introducing solids
- Finding a preschool
- Toilet training
- Positive discipline
- Readying your baby for toddlerhood
- Photographing your baby

The classes and workshops in your community may differ, as will the cost, but most offer at least a few of these and some offer more. What you should know is that you can feel a lot of pressure to get the best, up-to-the-minute advice and information. A class held at a reputable organization and taught by an experienced instructor can be the greatest investment you make, especially if you are a first-time parent who doesn't have a lot of people to ask questions of or if you simply want objective, professional advice. If taking parenting classes is what you want to do, see if you can make it fit in your budget.

If you would rather learn on your own and in the comfort of your own home, you may choose to invest in a few parenting books. Virtually every new mother and father has at least one. You can save some money and check out the selection at your local library, or if you plan on buying them, factor that additional cost into your budget. Each how-to guide will set you back approximately $10 to $18.

COVERING MEDICAL COSTS

Our nation is in the middle of a genuine health care crisis that has turned into a financial nightmare for many people. Just over half of all Americans filing for bankruptcy do so because of medical bills. A significant portion of those who seek debt assistance do so because they owe large sums of money to their doctor or hospital. Often, the money owed finds its way onto credit cards. Many times, such debts are with a collection agency, and can be extremely difficult to overcome.

As costly as it can be, health insurance is a necessary expense. Without it, the exorbitant cost of medical care will break all but the wealthiest of us. Make no mistake, medical costs in America are excessive, and all projections are that they will continue to skyrocket. Even if you have insurance, the price to keep you and the rest of your family healthy can be almost beyond comprehension.

If you are currently pregnant and worried about your insurance coverage because you need or want to change insurance plans, know that federal law—the Health Insurance Portability and Accountability Act (HIPPA) —protects you to at least some extent. If you change group health plans while you're pregnant, most of the time your new group health insurer cannot deny your pregnancy-related claims. As long as the plan includes maternity coverage, group health plans cannot exclude coverage for prenatal care or your baby's delivery, whether you are the primary insured or a dependent. In other words, health plans can't deny you coverage when you go from one job to another and switch employer-sponsored group health plans.

HIPAA doesn't apply to individual health plans, and if you switch from one individual policy to another, you might not get pregnancy coverage at all, or a waiting period may apply. If you purchase insurance while you are pregnant, you may find it tremendously expensive. However, because being covered with health insurance is so very important, you need to look at and assess all options. For more information about HIPPA, contact

- Office for Civil Rights
  U.S. Department of Health and Human Services
  Room 509F, HHH Building
  200 Independence Avenue SW
  Washington, DC 20201
  866-627-7748
  www.hhs.gov/ocr/

COBRA

To bridge the gap between health plans, you may be able to enroll in your former employer's plan for up to 18 months or until a new employer's plan kicks in. If you're between jobs, you may continue coverage with your previous employer under the Consolidated Omnibus Budget Reconciliation Act of 1985 (COBRA).

Basically, this means that you can keep the insurance plan you had, as long as you pay the same premium that your employer does. If your employer has 20 employees or more, it is required to offer COBRA (some states have laws similar to COBRA that apply to employers who have fewer than 20 employees). Keep in mind that premiums can be quite expensive. According to Families USA, a nonprofit organization dedicated to helping Americans obtain affordable health insurance, the current national average cost of COBRA coverage is $7,194 per year (about $600 per month) plus a 2 percent service fee. If you are pregnant, though, and you can't get insured any other way, the cost is almost always worth it.

Your employer is first required to notify you of your COBRA rights. Then you'll be mailed the necessary paperwork, and you'll have exactly 60 days to enroll by filling it out and sending it in. After that, you have 45 days to pay the first premium.

For more information about your rights under COBRA, contact

- U.S. Department of Labor
  Frances Perkins Building
  200 Constitution Avenue NW
  Washington, DC 20210
  866-444-3272
  www.dol.gov

Individual Health Insurance

If you are not covered by group health insurance through your employer and do not qualify for a government assistance insurance plan, it is important that you find some way to add insurance coverage to your budget. It can be difficult, but if you do your research, you may find a deal that you can afford. Many times, a health maintenance organization (HMO) has the least expensive premiums. Alternatively, you may pursue a policy with a high deductible—the amount you're responsible for *before* the insurer begins to pay. The higher the deductible, the lower the premiums. Any insurance is better than none, but if you or your baby does have a medical crisis, you can easily be out thousands of dollars with a high-deductible plan.

Health Savings Accounts

If you do have a high-deductible health insurance plan, you can plan for the cost of the deductibles and other uncovered costs with a health savings account (HSA), if one is available to you. These tax-advantaged accounts allow you to save for certain medical costs, including pregnancy and maternity expenses, while greatly reducing the amount you have to pay for some medical expenses.

If you buy the policy on your own, you can sign up for the HSA at various financial institutions, including banks, credit unions, and insurance companies. Your insurance agent should also be able to help guide you toward policies that qualify for HSAs. If you have group health insurance coverage through your employer and it qualifies as high-deductible, you will be able to sign up for an HSA during your open enrollment period. Your employer may even fund all or a portion of the HSA (and if it is particularly generous, they may even match contributions).

When you contribute to these accounts, you reduce your taxable income. Withdrawals and investment earnings are tax-free as long as you use the money for qualified health care costs. Not only that, but whether you itemize or take the standard deduction, you can deduct your HSA contributions on your income taxes. To use an HSA, your policy must have a specific deductible, but the law changes each year, so check with the IRS for account limit information. In addition, you can't be enrolled in Medicare, be covered by another health insurance policy that isn't a qualified high-deductible plan, or be claimed as a dependent on someone else's tax return. There is no "use it or lose it" rule, but there are maximum annual contribution limits and spending limits.

Again, check with the IRS for annual regulations:

- Internal Revenue Service
  800-829-1040
  www.irs.gov

Key Questions to Ask Your Insurance Company

To plan effectively for upcoming costs, you have to do a little investigative reporting. Be sure to ask your insurer the following questions:

- What types of medical care and medical professionals are covered?
- Are doulas, midwives, and pre- and postpartum home care covered?
- Will it cover all necessary blood work and other routine procedures?
- Are amniocentesis and other pregnancy-related testing covered?
- How much are prescription copayments, and for which medicines might you have to pay out of pocket?
- Are any parent education and childbirth classes covered?
- Are there any newborn care expenses that you will have to cover?
- Is lactation support, education, and assistance covered?
- Are there additional costs that you would be responsible for if your baby is born prematurely or with medical complications?

Extras, Extras, Read All About Them!

There are an untold number of other "health and well-being" costs associated with pregnancy and postpartum life. Here are just a few extras to consider adding to your list of expenses.

Three-Dimensional Images. Sure you will get to see hazy black-and-white ultrasound photographs while you have your appointments, but you can also pay for more enhanced images and videos of your developing baby. Want to have a three-dimensional photograph or video of your fetus? Then join those who are paying for the privilege of a preview by having a souped-up ultrasound. These are often done at separate clinics, although your hospital or birthing center may offer them as well. Many of these companies are franchises. The cost ranges, of course, but at one larger company right now, you can get a set of four-color, 3-D ultrasound photographs plus a few black-and-whites, a videotape of your ultrasound "experience," and a few extras, such as gender determination and an estimate of the fetal heart rate, for between $150 and $175.

Cord Blood Banking. Some parents choose to have their baby's umbilical cord blood cryogenically stored for use if their child becomes sick and needs a bone marrow transplant. Many different companies do this, all with different fee structures, but in general, the price begins at around $1,200 for collection of the cord blood and then $95 per year for storage. It is saved for up to 21 years, meaning the total cost would be about $3,000. Some companies allow you to prepay for storage at a discount of a few hundred dollars.

Doulas. You may want to have a neutral third-party professional, such as a doula, to coach you before and during your labor and delivery. Many also perform follow-up visits, where they come to your home and help you set up your space. Some women find them to be the best money they ever spent, particularly first-timers who want to be sure they have someone "on their side" and working exclusively for them. Keep in mind that the total fee for a doula is rarely covered by health insurance policies, but if you are interested, find out if and to what extent yours does. Doulas typically charge several hundred dollars.

For more information about doulas, contact the nonprofit organization Doulas of North America (DONA) at

- DONA International
  P.O. Box 626
  Jasper, IN 47547
  888-788-3662
  www.DONA.org
  info@DONA.org

PREPARING FOR LABOR AND DELIVERY COSTS

Whether you have insurance or not, you may be responsible for at least some of the expenses associated with childbirth. Among the many factors that go into how much you may have to pay are where you live, where you have your baby, whether or not you have insurance, what type of coverage you have, and whether you have a simple labor and delivery or one that is more complicated. As always, the earlier you prepare to face these upcoming issues and costs, the better.

Hospital Births

Hospitals are, by far, the most common places for childbirth, and they can also be the most expensive. Take for example, the 2005 labor and delivery hospital fees for a medical center in Sioux Falls, South Dakota (Figure 5.2).

If you want to have a pre- and postdelivery private room at the hospital, you may have to pay extra for it. That privilege can cost a few hundred dollars. Ask your insurance carrier or the hospital's financial department beforehand so you know what to expect.

Home Birth

Having your baby at home with a midwife can be a more economical alternative, and some insurance carriers do cover the associated costs. Because you aren't paying for a room or hospital stay, which can be a major childbirth expense, the costs are really minimized. In fact, according to the American Pregnancy Association, the average uncomplicated vaginal birth costs about 60 percent less in a home than in a hospital. Midwives are rarely covered by health insurance, however, and the typical fees range from $2,500 to $5,000.

Figure 5.2 *Labor and Delivery Fees Chart*

UNCOMPLICATED VAGINAL DELIVERY			
	Minimum	**Average**	**Maximum**
Charge	$2,187	$5,806	$46,342
Length of stay (in days)	1	2.2	31
Out-of-pocket (with coverage)*	0	$437	$5,080
Out-of-pocket** without coverage	0	$1,212	$4,380
UNCOMPLICATED CESAREAN SECTION			
	Minimum	**Average**	**Maximum**
Charge	$7,127	$11,633	$60,524
Length of stay (in days)	1	3.5	48
Out-of-pocket (with coverage)*	0	$518	$3,980
Out-of-pocket** without coverage	0	$1,317	$5,267

* Out-of-pocket with coverage reflects the amount a patient has paid to the hospital after insurance and/or government program (Medicare, Medicaid, etc.) payments are applied. The amount a patient paid was influenced by their insurance coverage, the timing of their hospitalization in conjunction with their insurance coverage, their willingness to provide information to qualify for financial assistance, and their ability to pay some or their entire obligation on a timely basis.

** Out-of-pocket without coverage reflects the amount a patient has paid to the hospital in the event they are not eligible for government programs (Medicare, Medicaid, etc.) and do not have health insurance coverage. The amount these patients paid was influenced by their willingness to provide information to qualify for financial assistance and their ability to pay some or their entire obligation on a timely basis.

Source: Sanford Health, 1305 W. 18th Street, PO Box 5039, Sioux Falls, SD 57117-5039

Birthing Center

Using a birthing center instead of a hospital is another option. Many women like them because they tend to have a homey, warm atmosphere as well as being a cost-effective option. In many cases, the average total fee for maternity care by a nurse-midwife and birth center facility is less than half the cost of a doctor and hospital delivery. Each birthing center has its own rates, but to get a feel for the average cost range, the Birth and Women's Center in Irving, Texas, charges around $4,500 if you aren't insured for maternity benefits, while the fees run a couple of thousand dollars higher at the Alma Birth center in Portland, Oregon.

No Insurance Options

Health insurance is an integral part of most American's budgets. As noted, the cost of medical care without it can break even the best-laid financial plan. However, the sad fact is that tens of millions of people in America do not have it and can't get it for various reasons. If you fall into this category and are due to have a baby, you need to contact your hospital and speak with one of their financial counselors as quickly as possible. Explain your situation and make a request to set up a pre-paid childbirth package. The sooner you do this, the better. If you can manage to pay for the labor and delivery before you actually have your baby, you can save a tremendous amount of money. In many cases, the package rate for a normal vaginal delivery is around $5,000. If you have to have a cesarean section or the birth is more complicated, you will be billed for the difference.

Beware of Insurance Scams

Unquestionably, health insurance can be a major expense. In fact, traditional policies may be out of your range completely. However, if you are tempted by the enticing ads for "discount" insurance plans, be careful. They typically promise comprehensive benefits for your entire family for a fraction of what you were quoted by a legitimate insurance company, no matter your age or health issues, but you may not get much for what you pay for. Most of the time, any coverage you get from these plans is thin at best. Although their marketing and advertisements can sound like they are insurance policies, they aren't, and they often do not provide adequate protection.

These discount health plans typically have a list of providers (doctors and other medical professionals) to whom you can go for treatment with whom they have negotiated discounted medical fees. Some exaggerate the savings potential, and others have been known to promise nonexistent discounts. Furthermore, the monthly fee is often heavy with administrative costs. Worst of all, some of these are flat-out scams and may go out of business during your participation, leaving you with nothing. It is important to do your research and be careful. If you have questions about these plans or feel as if you have been scammed, contact

- Federal Trade Commission
  600 Pennsylvania Avenue NW
  Washington, DC 20580
  877-FTC-HELP (382-4357)
  www.ftc.gov

Government Assistance

If your income is very low, you may qualify for Medicaid. This is a federal benefits program that is administered by each state, so what is covered and what isn't can vary considerably. This type of medical insurance is only available to certain low-income individuals and families who meet specific requirements—and thankfully pregnant women are listed as one of the eligibile groups. To know if you are eligible and to obtain information on your state's coverage and on signing up, contact

- U.S. Department of Health and Human Services
  Centers for Medicare and Medicaid Service
  7500 Security Boulevard Baltimore, MD 21244
  800-MEDICARE (633-4227)
  www.cms.hhs.gov

Copayments and Other Medical Costs

Don't forget, your medical expenses will likely continue after childbirth, often in the form of copayments and follow-up visits. Sure, they may only be $10 to $25 per visit, but those costs can really add up! This doesn't include all the prescriptions and other medications you may need to buy for normal health-related issues. Therefore, when you construct your budget, be sure to add in an average figure for copayments and other medical costs.

Bringing baby home, by whatever means you decide upon, can be taxing on your finances. Factor in everything discussed in this chapter, and you'll begin to realize why having a new baby is such an expensive endeavor. The key with these expenses is to know what they are, prioritize and plan for them, and reduce expenses where you can. Don't skimp on health care. Being financially covered now can save you from financial ruin tomorrow. I've seen it happen too many times not to give a proper heads-up.

CHAPTER SUMMARY

- Know the potential costs for the wide variety of fertility and adoption costs so you can consider each and devise an informed plan for which one(s) you want to pursue.
- Consider the benefits and expenses of parent education classes carefully.
- Understand your health insurance coverage:
  - Understand the potential benefits and drawbacks of each type of coverage.
  - Know what it covers and what it doesn't.
  - Plan for the costs that are not covered.
  - Communicate with your provider so there are no surprises.
  - Make insurance premiums a priority.
  - Add insurance copayments into your budget.

Chapter 6

Under Pressure

Where to Save and Where to Splurge

A LMOST ALL NEW PARENTS are at least somewhat unsure about what they *really* need to buy for their baby and what they can do without. Unfortunately, polling friends and family members can only heighten the uncertainty because everyone has their own opinion on what they couldn't live without not to mention having radically different financial situations. Therefore, if you are in the "What on earth should I buy?" stage, take heart. There is a way to prioritize shopping based on your own unique needs, style, and income.

PRESSURE TO SPEND

The message that many new parents hear, whether from internal voices or shouts from others, is clear: This is the time to splurge, to spend on all the special things that you and your new baby deserve. Don't be cheap, mom and dad. Make sure you have the most stylish and pampered kid

---

BABY SPENDING IS UP!

The U.S. retail market for infant, toddler, and preschool products (known in the industry by the acronym ITP) has been growing at a very healthy pace. According to the market research firm Packaged Facts, sales from 2004 to 2005 showed impressive growth:

- Home furnishings and accessories rose 5.2 percent to more than $8 billion.
- Toys were up 3.5 percent to $4.6 billion.
- Clothing and footwear were up 4.5 percent to nearly $16.8 billion.

---

in your neighborhood. Everyone around you is lavishing their little one with the finest money can buy, and you want to purchase only the basics? Oh no. No, no, no. You and your baby need to be fabulous—an entire family of fashionistas, if you will.

One of the most interesting things I found when I was counseling was how many people wanted to know how bad others had it as well as what the "haves" were getting. What are those who go all out getting their children?

- $50 Swarovski crystal pacifier
- $450 leather diaper bag
- $800 Egyptian cotton crib bedding
- $900 "Jester Heirloom" rocking horse
- $9,500 child's Mercedes 500 SL toy car
- $38,000 chalet-style playhouse
- $50,000 replica of Cinderella's coach for a toddler bed

Of course, the irony here is that it is not just the extremely wealthy who are buying these things for their precious progeny but some whose aim it is to one-up others in the neighborhood. Few of us are immune to social pressures, and just seeing pregnant coworkers sporting stylish maternity clothes and the vast number of toys other babies are playing with can make you feel inadequate if your baby doesn't have the same things or better. Before you go on a wild spending spree, put down those credit cards! This is actually the worst time to start, or continue, reckless spending. This unique juncture in your life is the very best time to *save* money and get into the habit of mindful purchasing. You are already undergoing significant life changes right now, so using this time of flux to adopt healthy and grounded financial practices just makes good sense.

You're likely experiencing other pressures as well. With your baby just arriving or on the way, you're probably feeling some nervousness and anxiety. Getting everything prepared for your new arrival is hard work, and trying to make key financial decisions in the middle of everything else that's going on can be particularly stressful. You want so much to do right by your baby, but it's difficult to know for sure what that means. New parents often feel a tremendous amount of fear that if they don't get certain things for their child, then there will be trouble down the road: baby won't be properly stimulated without the specially designed black-and-white mobile, or baby's skin will peel off in layers without the specially formulated baby-friendly laundry soap.

> **READ THE COPY!**
>
> "Tired of passing duplicate outfits on the playground or at the playgroup? . . . You will always find the perfect little something to spoil that bundle of joy in your life."
>
> —Advertising copy for a children's clothes store

If this sounds like you, to keep it together, you need to keep in mind that these fears are quite common and that you are likely worrying too much. As long as you use your common sense, make careful, informed choices, and are giving your baby all the love and care you can (all free of charge), you should be fine. Maintain a healthy perspective and find the inner discipline to resist spending pressures. Overcome the pangs of guilt that you may feel if some precious items are out of your current financial range. As you'll soon discover, your baby needs so very little of what the world is selling.

Of course, it is crucial to keep your baby safe and protected, and I would never dream of recommending that you not purchase items that help you achieve that goal, but do keep in mind that safety gear for your baby is a huge business whose goal is to get you spend as much of your hard-earned money as possible. More items get added to the "must-have" list every day, from cheap rubber sleeves you put on your bathtub faucet to expensive carbon monoxide detectors, and if you give in to every urge telling you that you simply must have *everything* for your baby, you'll likely find yourself in serious debt before long.

By far, my favorite source for checking up on which products and services are necessary and useful is *Consumer Reports*. On the website is an entire section dedicated to babies and kids. There you can peruse objective assessments of all sorts of things you may be considering buying. It will certainly help you make sound decisions about what you can be frugal with and what might be better to spend a bit more on. Log on to *www.consumerreports.org* to review the latest research on a wealth of common baby items.

Marketing to Parents

How is it that when you go shopping, you sometimes spend so much more money than you intend to? Remember, you're being pulled in a lot of different directions right now, so you may not have your best judgment at your disposal. In addition, don't forget, selling to expecting and new parents is more extreme and aggressive than ever. In fact, some companies are wholly focused on making sure that you, as a new parent, will spend as much of your money on the latest and greatest baby gear as possible. Because you are in the process of shopping for a whole new set of items, you are a highly desirable (and if you're not careful, susceptible) customer. It's easy to fall under the spell of those who are doing their best to get you to part ways with your hard-earned money. The key is getting you to believe that if you just had this or that great new item, you'd be a superior mother or father. I have seen over and over again how parents overbuy based on image, labels, and hype—and I've seen the resulting debt, too.

It can be very hard to sift through the hype of what you really need versus what you really want—and what advertisers and the media say you should want. Right now, you really have to keep your wits about you by being a conscious, mindful shopper. Let your guard down, and you very well may find yourself swiping your credit card at a frenzied pace. When shopping for maternity and parenting items, always be conscious of why

Figure 6.1 *Baby Stroller Cost Comparison Chart*

BABY STROLLER COST COMPARISON CHART				
Price Range	Umbrella	Traditional	Jogger	Total
Low	Jeep all-weather reclining umbrella stroller $40	Combi Cosmo ST Caribbean standard stroller $60	Kolcraft Contours Options 3-wheeler jogger stroller $130	$230
Mid	Chicco C6 umbrella stroller: $60	Peg Perego Aria MT—Rubino standard stroller $170	Mutsy Spider jogger stroller $250	$480
High	Maclaren Volo umbrella stroller $120	Mountain Buggy urban single standard stroller $420	Regal Lager E3 jogger stroller $350	$890
Luxury	Inglesina Zippy AN5 Rame umbrella stroller $340	Stokke Xplory standard stroller $800	Quinny Buzz jogger stroller $500	$1,640

Average costs based on April 2007 figures. Many parents have an umbrella stroller that folds up easily and can live in the trunk of the car, a standard stroller for everyday use, and a jogging stroller for exercising with baby. Features, overall quality, and aesthetics range between makes and models, but they all do the same basic thing—transport your child.

you choose one product over another. Ask yourself if it is the packaging, the promises, the price, or something else. This quick dialogue will help you become active and analytical with your buying decisions, which will then help you reduce impulse buys and make more carefully considered and informed purchases.

Figure 6.1 provides a good look at how much the price of a common baby item (a baby stroller) can vary and why it's so important to shop smartly. To know what stroller meets your needs and financial parameters, make an educated decision after assessing the benefits and drawback of each make and model.

The $1,000 Stroller. Seeing what other families have can give you many great, and not so great, ideas about what you'd like to have for your baby, too. By far the most dramatic example of this is the luxury stroller. It is easy to spot. I call it the $1,000 stroller, because fully loaded, that is about what it costs. When you see other parents in your neighborhood pushing a posh baby-carting device, you may very well want one, too.

However, ask yourself a few questions first. Should you get one, do you need one, and is it really worth half your monthly paycheck? What you choose to spend money on is up to you, of course, but if you're going to buy it, do so because you really love it and have the cash to spend, not because someone else up the block has one or that you'll be the only parent pushing an economy model if you don't get it. Let's remember that a purchase like this has very little to do with your baby's needs and everything to do with your value system.

Separating necessity from luxury can get confusing, which is why I recommend taking a few moments *before* racing to the cash register to consider carefully whether or not the item you are about to buy provides any real benefit to your baby. Your wallet will thank you for the few extra minutes of rational thought.

ALL YOU NEED IS LOVE (AND A FEW MORE THINGS)

Here's the wonderful truth: there's very little that you'll actually need to buy to ensure the safety and happiness of your newborn. All that's really needed is love, food, and shelter. Love is free, of course. If you are or will be breast-feeding, you won't have to pay for formula. That leaves shelter. Your baby won't know if she's living in a shack or a mansion, not until she's a bit older anyway. Sure, your baby need clothes and a few other basics as well (I've never met a parent who didn't make constant use of those rubber bulb syringes to keep their baby's nose clear, and those harnessed bouncing seats are unbelievably convenient, for example), but the point is that in the beginning of your baby's life, the actual necessities are few. Don't beat yourself up if you can't afford the special black-and-white mobile that we're told is "vital" for your baby's hand-eye-brain-aesthetic development. The baby will be okay. You'll be okay. As a new parent, you have enough to worry about without adding shopping anxiety to your plate.

BREAST-FEEDING: A GREAT WAY TO SAVE

Not everyone can or wants to breast-feed baby. However, if you break it down into economic terms, nursing makes a lot of financial sense. Formula feeding be expensive:

Cost of Formula and Bottles:
Per Month Cumulative Nursing Savings*

1	$102	5	$567	9	$1,062
2	$196	6	$691	10	$1,186
3	$320	7	$815	11	$1,309
4	$443	8	$938	12	$1,433

Figures include the average cost of brands of premixed and powdered formula available in stores Northampton, Massachusetts, and the purchase of four bottles and nipples every two months.

THE AVERAGES: FIRST YEAR BABY COSTS

A baby's initial "start-up costs" are only the beginning. After all, you're only going to buy one crib, right? You may have other regular and occasional monthly expenses to add into your budget, too. Here's an overview of some new cost considerations for baby's first year:

Child Care

Whether you are going back to work or just in need of the occasional date-night getaway, many people have to pay for some sort of child care on a somewhat regular basis. A once-a-month babysitter may set you back $40–$60. Full-time day care may be $600 a month. Chapter 10, "All About Child Care: Types, Facts, and Costs," will provide you with more detailed information about what your child care expenses may be.

Clothing and Shoes

On average, American parents spend roughly $600 dressing their baby in the first year, meaning the monthly cost is somewhere around $50. Don't forget that this is one of those areas where using the resources you have available to you, from friends and family to garage sales and bargain racks, can really make a difference in your budget.

THE WIC PROGRAM

If you're seriously stressed out about how you're going to pay for even the basics, you may be eligible for a program that can reduce some of the financial pressure. It is called WIC, which stands for Women, Infants, Children. This federally funded program is for low-income pregnant, postpartum, and breast-feeding women and infants and children up to age five who are at nutrition risk. It provides you with either checks or vouchers so you can buy nutritiously sound food, including such staples as infant formula, cereal, juice, eggs, milk, cheese, peanut butter, dried beans, tuna fish, and carrots. You can even get special therapeutic infant formulas and medical foods, if they've been prescribed by your doctor.

To qualify for WIC, your income must fall at or below 185 percent of the U.S. Poverty Income Guidelines (currently $35,798 for a family of four), meet a state residency requirement, and are determined to be at "nutrition risk" by a health professional. You automatically qualify if you participate in certain other government benefit programs. To learn more about WIC, contact

- WIC at Food and Nutrition Headquarters
  Supplemental Food Programs Division
  Food and Nutrition Service—USDA
  3101 Park Center Drive
  Alexandria, VA 22302
  (703) 305-2746
  www.fns.usda.gov/wic/

Diapers

Ah, diapers. You will be mighty familiar with them soon, if you aren't already. If you can buy them in bulk and are committed to locating the best deal, the cost will be somewhere around $40 per month. However, if you have to duck into a convenience store on a somewhat regular basis to buy them, you'll likely pay a lot more. Many parents choose cloth or save money by sewing their own diapers or buying them on eBay. This may surprise some of you, but lots of people do this, and after an initial outlay of a couple of hundred dollars, it's much cheaper in the long run. In most cases, a cloth diaper service will be about as expensive as buying disposables.

Formula

If you aren't going to be making your own baby food, an economical choice that simply requires nursing or pumping, you'll be buying
formula. The amount this will cost varies tremendously, depending on
brand, type, and your baby's needs. On average though, formula will run
you somewhere between $100 and $150 per month. As baby begins to
eat solid food, it will be less, of course.

Not everyone can or wants to breast-feed their baby. However, if
you break it down into economic terms, nursing makes a lot of financial
sense. Clearly, formula and bottles can be expensive.

Food

Starting at around six months, your baby will be eating real food! If
you aren't going to make your own baby food, probably an economical
choice that simply requires mashing or grinding your own meals to an
unappetizing pulp, you may be buying jarred food and boxes of baby
cereal. It will only be a few dollars a day, but on a monthly basis, you are
looking at approximately $75.

WHAT YOU "NEED"

As previously mentioned, there really is very little that you and your baby
must have in the beginning. That said, many useful items can be quite
useful and make your family's life much easier and more enjoyable. As
you consider each one, ask yourself how much use you'll likely get out of
it and whether or not it's worth the cost. In other words, you won't need a
jogging stroller if you are not going to be taking baby out for runs, so why
waste your money? That may sound obvious, but countless baby joggers
are taking up space in garages and closets across the country. As with all of
your purchases, err on the side of being realistic rather than hopeful.

A quick note of caution: beware of "list mania." It has become routine for new parents to rely heavily on the Internet to get terrific, up-to-
the-minute information and guidance. However, because each website,
forum, and chat room provides varying perspectives on what is a required
item, it can get more than a little confusing, so be careful.

Figure 6.2 shows just one of the many anonymously written,
must-have baby-preparation lists available online. I'd say it's pretty

Figure 6.2 *New Baby Essentials*

NEW BABY ESSENTIALS		
1. Bassinet	34. Receiving blankets	69. Portable crib
2. Crib	35. Socks	70. Pillow
3. Humidifier	36. Shoes	71. Diaper bag
4. Bed sheets	37. Infant sit-up chair	72. Stroller
5. Picture frames	38. Tub	73. Sunshade
6. Baby musical CDs	39. Cotton swabs	74. Safety gate
7. Small radio/ CD player	40. Baby oil	75. Outlet covers
8. Bumper pads	41. Vaseline	76. Carbon monoxide detector
9. Mobile	42. Bathtub	77. Supermarket cart cover
10. Wall decor	43. Baby shampoo	78. Corner covers
11. Nursery monitor	44. Baby lotion	79. Door knob covers
12. Changing table	45. Bath sponge	80. Cabinet locks
13. Crib mattress	46. Bath toys	81. Swing
14. Night light	47. Washcloths	82. Play mat
15. Dresser	48. Nail clippers	83. Stuffed animals
16. Teddy bears & dolls	49. Potty chair	84. Walkers
17. Changing pad for home	50. Brush/Comb	85. Bouncy chair
18. Changing pad for travel	51. Baby wipes	86. Toy box
19. Rocker/Glider	52. Bottle cleaning brush	87. Toys
20. Ottoman	53. Bottle warmer	88. Baby rocker
21. Baby lamp	54. Baby Cereal	89. Foam floor padding
22. Shelves	55. Formula	90. Jolly Jumper
23. Chest	56. Nursing pillow	91. Educational DVDs
24. T-Shirts	57. High chair	92. Books
25. Sleepers	58. Breast pump	93. Custom website or online album
26. Bodysuits	59. Baby bowl	94. Digital camera
27. Jackets	60. Bottle drying rack	95. Photo albums
28. Diapers	61. Feeding spoons	96. Video camera
29. Pants	62. Bottle sterilizer	97. Tripod
30. Sweaters	63. Bottles	
31. Hats	64. Wipes	
32. Mittens	65. Wipes warmer	
33. Undershirts	66. Bibs	
	67. Plates	
	68. Car seat	

comprehensive—and a bit exhausting to read. Buy it all, and you may have to remortgage your home. Certainly, many of these items are practical and can make your life comfortable and pleasurable. However, many of them may not fit your routine in the slightest, rendering them useless, not to mention a complete waste of money.

Use the baby basics worksheet (Figure 6.3) to help you determine what you think you'll need and like to have for your newborn. It gives a rundown of most of the things that new families need to get started. Keep in mind that the prices for these items can vary considerably, depending on such variables as where you live and where you'll be shopping, so it's worth your time to track down the best bargains available. Before you walk into just any store and start buying, do yourself a favor and research the best price, either online or in your local newspaper and catalogs or just ask around—other new parents are often the greatest resource for tips on where the bargains are.

When you have a good idea of what these items will cost, write it down and calculate the grand total to figure out how much you'll need to budget for these things. Although the items focus mainly on the newborn period, feel free to add to your list as you go along.

There are approximately 32 items listed on the worksheet, a far cry from the nearly 100 on the sample list that was found floating around the Internet. You'll notice that I didn't include any toys, stuffed animals, decorations, and the like. The clothes that are included in the necessary items list are limited to essentials, too. Most new parents have the same observation about a baby's first few months—they don't wear a lot. Newborns *live* in onesies, a pair of socks, and maybe a hat.

Once you have reviewed everything and decided what you would like to buy, add any additional necessities that weren't included, calculate the total cost, and see how you can make it fit within your current budget. Decide how you're going to pay for it all. Do you have the cash for everything you want, or are you going to need to charge some and repay the balance over the next couple of months? Can you prioritize and buy a few items now and a few later? Can any of these items be put on your baby shower (if you have one) registry, so you don't have to pay for everything yourself? Be sure to prioritize what you want by determining what you feel you can live without and what you can't. Naturally, as your

Figure 6.3 *Baby Basics Worksheet*

		BABY BASICS WORKSHEET			
Need	**Item**	**Initial Quantity**	**Comment**	**Price**	
	Undershirts	12	These are pretty much required items, but thankfully they can be had for next to nothing. Buy in bulk, at least three to a package.		
	"Onesies" (the little bodysuits with snaps at the bottom)	At least 12	See above.		
	Socks or booties	12	See above.		
	Footed pajamas	6 to 12	See above.		
	Hats	2	See above.		
	Blankets in varying weights for warmth	6 to 10 (more if your baby is a spitter-upper)	The hospital may provide at least a few for free.		
	Diapers— disposable	A few packages	Newborns go through about 6–10 a day.		
	Diaper disposal system	1	For some they are vital; for other's they are a waste.		
	Diapers—cloth (including covers and closures)	24; 12 covers; 7–8 Velcro closures	If you will be using a delivery service, you won't have to buy any. The company will help you figure out what you need and the cost.		
	Diaper bag	1	You can get away with using just any old large handbag, but bags made especially for diapers and other infant gear can be a great convenience.		
	Baby wipes	A few boxes	Soft, moistened paper towels will do, too, but the difference in cost doesn't usually outweigh the convenience.		

Figure 6.3 *Baby Basics Worksheet (continued)*

Need	Item	Initial Quantity	Comment	Price
	Car seat	I	The most expensive is not always the best. Check in consumer magazines for prices versus quality.	
	Baby monitor	I	If your home is particularly large and you won't be cosleeping	
	Baby nail clippers/scissors manicure set	I	You'll be surprised at how fast those nails grow (and scratch baby's face).	
	Stroller	I–2	As with the car seat, there are many models to choose from. Research price and features carefully.	
	Soft baby carrier	I	Whether it is a sling or a front or back soft baby holder, these are invaluable for walks and comfort.	
	Sleeping "area": crib or bassinette	I	If you are going to be using a crib, that is. Not necessary if you will be cosleeping.	
	Crib linens/ sheet sets	3–4 sets	The number you need depends on how often you do laundry. Some babies spit up a lot meaning you'll need a few extra sets.	
	Portable crib	I	Totally unnecessary if you plan on staying put. Very useful if you travel.	
	Bouncy seat	I	Most parents find these invaluable (I did). These "infant chairs" are at a nice angle for baby. Expensive models vibrate, less expensive ones don't.	
	Changing table		Some swear by a designated changing table. Others (like me) were fine with a dresser top with a pad.	

(continued)

Figure 6.3 *Baby Basics Worksheet (continued)*

Need	Item	Initial Quantity	Comment	Price
	Portable changing pad	1	Excellent for playgrounds, restaurants, etc.	
	Dresser	1	If you don't already have a spare, you're going to have to put baby's clothes somewhere. Hint: Don't go crazy with baby furniture. A four-year-old may not be too happy with the image of leaping bunnies.	
	Clothes hamper	1	A box will do, so you can definitely go cheap on this one. You just don't want dirty things strewn about the floor. Chances are the laundry will pile up anyway, but a designated drop spot is good.	
	Breast pump	1	If you will be nursing and want to express milk, pumps are important. You can rent high-quality ones from the hospital or birthing center or buy your own. (If you know you'll be having more children, this option makes sense.)	
	Nursing bras	1 to begin with	Nursing bras generally start at $25 but can be much more. Before you invest in a few, make sure you'll be in it for the long haul.	
	Bottles	2–8, depending on how often/rarely you'll be using the bottle	Necessary if you will be bottle feeding, either with formula or expressed breast milk	
	Formula	2 small containers—different varieties	This is tricky. Your baby may react negatively to a few different makes of formula, so buy a small container of one type and see how it goes.	

Figure 6.3 *Baby Basics Worksheet (continued)*

Need	Item	Initial Quantity	Comment	Price
	Rectal or digital ear thermometer	I	Yes, you'll need it. It's crazy how often you'll be reading that thermometer.	
	Bathtubs	I	Many parents get away without these plastic tubs (I never had one), but others consider them a necessity.	
	Diaper rash ointment	I	Almost all babies get a red and sore bottom. This is nice to have on hand and costs just a few dollars.	
	Bulb syringe	I	Sometimes the hospital will give this nose destuffer as a parting gift.	
Total Cost:				

baby grows, he will need a few more things. Some good baby fundamentals that are appropriate for most families are the following:

☐ One-piece outfits
☐ Footed sleepers
☐ T-shirts
☐ Leggings or pull-on pants
☐ Sweaters, sweatshirts, jackets
☐ Hats
☐ Mittens
☐ Socks or booties
☐ Shoes
☐ Another stroller
☐ Larger car seat
☐ High chair
☐ Plastic "sippy" cups, plates and bowls, and baby spoons
☐ Bibs

☐ Safety gate
☐ Outlet protectors
☐ Cupboard and drawer latches

It's a good idea to mark off those things that you think you may want to buy, prioritizing as you go forward. Remember, you don't have to get everything all at once, unless you spot an unusually great deal. In that case, try to take advantage of it while it lasts.

The Power of Preparation

Because you'll want to be prepared for your baby's arrival, you'll likely make some projections about what you're going to need. The key to doing this accurately is not to overbuy right now. There's a very good chance that some of the decisions you make about how you are going to raise your baby may not work out the way you had hoped, and you don't want to purchase a lot of expensive accoutrements only for them to go to waste. The following are a few really good examples of this.

Feeding. Whether you are 100 percent committed to feeding your baby breast milk or formula, many parents change their mind midway through. With both methods though, there are all sorts of associated gadgets. Nursing mothers may need breast pumps and special freezer bags to store expressed milk, and parents who can't or prefer not to nurse will need to purchase bottles and, of course, formula. Overall, breast-feeding is the less expensive alternative, but you never know what will work best for you until you're in the middle of it, so stay flexible.

Sleeping. I can't tell you how many parents I have spoken with who said that they never, *not once,* used their bassinette or crib. The baby slept with them until a bed of his own was necessary. On the flip side, a lot of parents had the intention of cosleeping from the beginning, only to come to the conclusion that separate sleeping arrangements worked better for them. Again, when your baby arrives, you'll have a much better idea about exactly what you and your baby will need.

Diapering. The majority of American parents choose disposable diapers for their baby, but there is a trend toward cloth, either buying your own and laundering them as in the good old days or hiring a delivery service where fresh, clean diapers come to you on a regular basis. Either way, there are some products that you should consider purchasing. If you use disposables you may need, or want, one of the special trash systems that whisk away the scent of soiled diapers; if you go for cloth, you're going to need a lot of diaper covers and closures.

What sounds great to you right now may not work in the end, so go easy and try to spend prudently. Wait and see what will work for you. There is so much expensive paraphernalia out there, and you don't want to waste your precious money on things that do nothing more than collect dust or make you feel guilty every time you see them. Don't worry; the stores will always be there. The products will always be sold, and if you really need them, you can get them later.

Getting the Gear

Once you have a good idea of what you and your baby will need, you have to figure out the best place to get these things. Shopping at high-end baby gear stores is a fun experience, but you'll be paying a premium for the basics—so let's focus on some of the places where you're most likely to snag a great bargain.

Superstores. Love or loathe those mega-emporiums, big box stores are where you can often find some of the most amazing deals. Some may say that they're completely devoid of charm, but once you compare the cost of their 12-pack of baby booties to the single pair you'll find at a small boutique, you may quickly get over the stark atmosphere. Superstores are where you'll likely save huge amounts of money on all sorts of baby supplies, from diapers to wipes and everything in-between. If you have ethical or political issues regarding the way these stores operate, don't shop there. Otherwise, make a run for it—your wallet will thank you!

Online Shopping. There are many online stores where you can shop for all of your baby needs and have your purchases delivered right to you. This can be rather helpful if you are pregnant and are having difficulty getting around. Another benefit of online shopping is that it's easy to compare prices—just a click of the mouse can usually get you an instant price comparison. It can also help you cut down on the impulse purchases that are so common when shopping for baby. Many people find it a lot easier to stick to their list when they aren't being tempted by eye-catching displays of other enticing items.

Before you buy online though, do a little research: Know the online store's refund policy, including the reimbursement time frame, shipping costs, and if there are any restocking fees. Some things just don't look as good in real life as they do on your computer monitor, and you may very well want to send them back.

Online auctions are also highly recommended for some items. You can often walk away with some amazing bargains, not to mention that bidding on what you want can be pretty exciting. Be careful though and listen to the following warning from eBay, the world's most popular auction website:

> Before buying an item, review the feedback that members have left for a seller, and learn about PayPal, eBay's preferred way to pay. Learning about a seller's past trading experiences will help you decide if this is a person you feel you can trust.

In addition, be sure to read the product's description carefully. Items described as *refurbished, vintage,* or *closeout* can mean that what you're buying isn't in a pristine state. Curiously, cheap prices on luxury goods may indicate counterfeit products.

Here's some more advice to those of you who are just entering the world of online shopping: credit cards rather than debit cards are ideal for purchasing because they offer built-in consumer protection. If what you bought doesn't arrive or isn't what you ordered, you can dispute the charge with your credit card company. In addition, never email your personal or financial information; use the company's website instead. Check to see if there's a lock icon on the browser's status bar, and the URL for the website should begin with *https*. Never let your guard down when shopping online: be careful!

Consignment and Secondhand Stores/Garage Sales. I can see new mothers and fathers cringing when they read these words, but this is where some of the most incredible deals can be had. Think about all of those parents who bought things for their baby that they either never or barely ever used! If you can get over the thought that the clothes were worn by another baby or that the furniture might have held another child's blankets, seriously consider buying used for at least a few expensive items. There's nothing wrong with capitalizing on other people's splurges.

As for garage sales, use your local newspaper, community bulletin boards and websites, and word of mouth to find out when the sales are going on in your area. The earlier you get to them, the better; lots of other people will be waiting to get there first and scoop up all the best bargains. I recommend looking for such items as books and washable toys. You'll pay literally next to nothing for things that initially cost quite a lot of money. For example, I once bought a huge box of children's books for 50 cents—there must have been 30 books in that magic cardboard box. The price of one book these days is easily $5, so I saved about $149.50.

Other Parents. Do you know someone who has already had children and who may have a fold-up crib or other perfectly good baby supplies in their attic? Depending on your relationship with them, don't be afraid to ask if you can have or borrow it. There are some things you simply won't need forever, so why buy them if you can borrow?

For me, this was maternity clothes. During my pregnancy, I knew of a few women who had recently had their babies. They did not need their supersized dresses and delightful panel-front jeans anymore, so they kindly passed them on to me. When I was done with them, I passed them on to other big-bellied women in need. Now, previously worn clothes may not appeal to you, but other things might. Although used items may not be your first choice, it makes good financial sense to save money where you can now, so more will be available when you need it later.

The Baby Shower. If you are going to have a baby shower, be sure to use it to your advantage. Many of the things you'll want to help set up your home for baby can be provided by your friends and loved ones. When planning for your shower, you may choose to register for the items you want or have a baby gift free-for-all. There's no clear consensus on which is best.

The benefits of registering, of course, are that you get to choose exactly what you want and all that your guests have to do is refer to the store directory. Many people love the ease that a preselected gift list offers, especially if they don't have children and haven't got a clue as to what a new family may desire. This doesn't mean you won't get surprises; some people just refuse to "conform" to your needs and taste. You'll get what they think is best—and sometimes they're right.

For some, registering for a baby shower is in poor taste and is simply not done in their community or group of friends. Of course, if you don't preselect, your guests will be free as birds to express their personality a bit more (hopefully, they're thinking about *you* and what you need and like). Be prepared for some rather interesting gifts, doubling up on items, and things that are completely useless for you. For example, I didn't register and received a baby monitor, which for most people would be a terrific and very practical gift. Unfortunately, our apartment was all of about 1,200 square feet, so it was completely unnecessary for us.

All things considered, the way you want to structure your baby shower, if you even want one at all, is your decision. There's no one right way, and don't let anyone pressure you into doing it the way they would. However, if you do have one, and register, do your friends and family a huge favor: include items that people on any budget can afford.

AND NOW FOR THE SPLURGES

Although it's important to adhere to a sensible budget, you don't have to deprive yourself and your baby completely. The basics are great, and you've got to have them, but there is more to parenting life than bottles and diapers. There are so many beautiful, practical, and fun products for parenting and baby that aren't essential but sure can make your job as a mother or father much easier and more enjoyable. Relaxing the purse strings for some nonessentials every once in a while, as long as it doesn't wreak havoc with paying your bills or impair saving for something you really need, is important. Parenting is hard work; you can and should enjoy the fruits of your labor, which includes both baby and money!

Maternity Splurges

Not just baby products pry precious dollars from your bank account. The very common desire to feel good and beautiful during pregnancy is a factor, too. High-end maternity wear and gear are commonplace now, and sales for such items are on the rise. In fact, Mothers Work, Inc., the world's leading maternity apparel retailer, reported record-breaking sales for 2007. According to a June 2006 article in the *New York Times*, sales for maternity wear increased by 28 percent between 2000 and 2005, while the overall women's clothing market showed a mere 2 percent increase during the same period.

The nine months of pregnancy can really be emotionally and physically rough on some women. A few products and services can make you feel a whole lot better. Some are huge splurges, while others are little indulgences, so it might make sense to choose items that make you feel good but don't put your finances in jeopardy.

A massage by a professional therapist who specializes in pregnant women may be the best $100 you ever wrote a check for. When you're pregnant your body is in overdrive, and it is easy to become sore and exhausted. A good massage will leave you revived and refreshed.

Many women report feeling like a movie star when pregnant . . . for about a month. To help with the other eight months, you may want to drop some cash for a few beautiful maternity outfits. A great, well-designed, well-proportioned dress that won't bind or ride up is usually worth the splurge. Manicures, pedicures, waxes, or a great haircut are all things that aren't critical but if you love these types of things, they may make your pregnancy that much more pleasant.

There is nothing wrong with wanting to look and feel amazing while you are pregnant, but assess your need before you splurge on those items. It can make sense to indulge on nonessentials if

- you have the money—the obvious answer;
- you are going to have another child or two and can use the items again;
- there is a specific need for it, and you can't get around purchasing it yourself; or
- you can't get by with more economical alternatives.

Feeding-Time Splurges

In the first year, you're going to be doing a tremendous amount of nursing or bottle-feeding. This means you are going to want to get comfortable. You may want to invest in a seriously cozy chair (there are special recliners for this purpose) along with a footstool. Sure the couch or bed will do, but you tend to be in a rather uncomfortable position for a long time, so consider investing in a more relaxing option.

To get in the right feeding position, whether you are nursing or bottle-feeding, investing in a specially designed pillow that fits on your lap can save you a fortune at the chiropractor later. Sure you can stuff a cushion between you and your baby, but these devices are ergonomically designed to get you in just the right arc for feeding.

I nursed my daughter for the first 13 months, and throughout the process, my dream was to have a minifridge at my feet stocked with ice-cold water to beat my unquenchable thirst. Looking back, I wonder why I didn't. Having a few additional creature comforts during your pregnancy can make all the difference in the world.

Baby Splurges

A few expensive plush outfits for your little one should satisfy your natural desire to spoil your baby and lavish him with all things grand. If you can afford it, go ahead and buy new designer duds; if you can't afford a whole new designer wardrobe, though, you may be able to get the same or similar gear at baby consignment stores. You can then take pictures of her in that outfit or dress that will last a lifetime.

Nice bedding for the baby is a great indulgence, too. Because he will sleep so much, it's a nice thought that your baby is laying his perfect little face on the softest of sheets.

Comfort is the key all around, and that includes getting around with baby. If you have the money, I suggest getting the best carrying device, the kind that you strap to your front so you can move around with the baby. These can be expensive, but the nicer ones are usually worth the price. Slings can be great, too, but many parents don't find a huge difference between those that are pricey and those that aren't.

"You" Time Splurges

Some parents can't be away from their little one for more than five minutes, while others need a break, sometimes a long one. If you don't have friends or family around who can relieve you from duty, think about hiring a babysitter. They can be expensive, but there's really no price you can put on your sanity. Chances are you aren't going to be sleeping a lot, so maybe you can pay someone to come in so you can get some uninterrupted sleep every now and then. You may crave some baby-free time with your partner or friends to enjoy a movie, dinner, or something not baby-related fun. Scheduling "you" time, even if you have to pay for it, is often vital to being a happy and fulfilled mother or father.

Going to Extremes

Of course it's possible to go to extremes, both in the extravagance and the frugality departments. I'm not immune to this, either; my years in the money management and debt reduction business, coupled with my natural penny-pinching tendencies, turned me into quite the savings fanatic while I was pregnant.

I'd ask my sister, who already had two children, for advice. "Do I really have to buy clothes for the baby?" I'd say. "Won't she just grow out of them fast, and then I'll have to buy more? Can't I just use a pillow case with armholes cut in the sides?"

Looking at me with alarm, and more than a little concerned for my sanity, she'd gently say, "Yes, you *can* do that . . . but why would you?"

I was probably being a bit over the top with my radical cost-cutting measures, and in the end, I did buy clothes for my daughter. However, I must say that the best outfits she wore came courtesy of my sister. There's nothing like hand-me-downs from someone who isn't afraid to spend money, and it's amazing what you can get away with by not spending—and still have a perfectly normal and enjoyable pre- and postpartum experience.

Choosing where and when to splurge and save can be tricky, especially when you have so much else going on in your life. A tremendous amount of baby products and services are available—just thinking about it all can leave you feeling overwhelmed. Make sure to try and strike a balance between what you need and what you want. Save wherever you can and splurge on what you love, all within reason. Remember, your baby really needs so little in the beginning. A few indulgences can go a long way toward satisfying your desire to spoil your baby.

CHAPTER SUMMARY

- Replace the "now is not the time to go cheap" attitude with "now is the time to be financially sensible."
- Be cautious of marketing's influence on your buying decisions—you are a very desirable and targeted market.
- Indulge in the finer things in life prudently.
- Remember how you want your child to think of money and behave the way you want him to eventually.
- Don't buy out of guilt. Buy *after* you've analyzed what you really need.
- *Never* try to keep up with your neighbors. It's a no-win game.
- Transform yourself into a conscious, mindful shopper. Why are you buying what they are selling? Is it the packaging, the promises, the price, or something else?
- Listen to other parents' recommendations and then assess them against your values, lifestyle, and financial circumstances.
- Make a careful distinction between what you need versus what you want for your baby and make sure the essentials are covered first.
- Recognize that you won't know everything that you're going to need for your baby all at once, so don't overbuy. Take a wait-and-see approach.
- When purchasing baby items, prioritize and find bargains wherever you can.
- If you do charge some items, make sure you can repay the entire balance in a couple of months at the most.
- Choose the right store or source to get the best deal on what you want.
- Remember your increased monthly expenses as you consider your baby start-up costs.
- Splurge prudently on the items and services that provide the most pleasure for the cost.

Chapter 7

On the Double

Partner Issues

WHAT ARE THE ODDS that two people, even if they love each other, will agree on all money issues? If you guessed very, very slim, you'd be right. Now, what is the probability that that same couple has completely identical attitudes about raising a child? Again, it's highly unlikely. Even if you and your partner were brought up under near-identical circumstances, it's doubtful that you share the same attitudes and habits about every issue. However, this is not an insurmountable situation. Contradictory opinions about money in new-parent couples is quite common. The key to overcoming these differences is encountering each issue with an open mind, honest communication, patience, and the knowledge that ultimately, both of you want the same thing—a happy and secure family. It won't always be easy, but healthy compromise on all money issues can be achieved.

Attitudinal differences may not be *too* big of a problem when it is just the two of you, but during pregnancy and after the baby arrives, a whole new set of contentious monetary issues often emerge. The regular financial demands of caring for a child can put quite a lot of pressure on new parents, and if you're having a tough time making ends meet now, then it probably isn't going to get any easier down the line. You're both likely to be exhausted taking care of your baby, making the patience and the energy to confront money issues in a healthy way scarce commodities. Furthermore, with everything else going on in your lives right now, what seemed crucial yesterday may not be so today. This can make planning for and achieving like-minded goals feel like an impossible task.

In most cases, it is not impossible. Having a baby can be a stressful but wonderful time in the lives of you and your partner. This is not the time to let issues regarding money come between you; you'll soon have enough to deal with, and your ability to work together needs to be at its strongest to make cohesive financial decisions that are in the best interest of your entire family. *Not* taking the time to address money matters, so you can get your finances in order, is a surefire recipe for conflict later.

Putting in the necessary effort to work out any money disagreements arise will allow you and your partner to focus on all the other baby issues you will encounter and to prepare for the future together. Again, this process involves a lot of honest and open communication, compromise, and commitment not to mention patience, good humor, and forgiveness. You will have to make an effort both to understand and be okay with each other's money value systems and eventually combine forces so you can achieve great things together. You may be surprised by what you find when you talk productively about these topics.

YOUR FAMILY FINANCES

If you and your partner haven't already come to an agreement on money issues, it's certainly within your best interest to do so as soon as possible. As parents, you both have an equal investment in the well-being of your child, whether one of you gets up to go to work in the morning and the other stays at home with the baby, or any number of working scenarios. You are a family and need to work effectively as one. This doesn't mean that you have to share absolutely everything. Do you need to have joint savings, checking, and credit accounts? No, but do you need to have compatible fundamental financial goals? Yes. To know for sure that you do, it's important to communicate with your partner.

The following money compatibility quiz is designed to make an initial assessment of your and your partner's level of agreement regarding money matters and to gauge your overall level of trust and comfort. After taking this quiz, you should have a good sense of how similar or different your feelings regarding money are and how much work you may have to do to bring your financial goals closer to a mutually agreeable middle ground.

QUIZ: Money Compatibility

Answer the following questions with a yes or no response. Choose the answer that best fits your overall feelings regarding you and your partner.

1. Are you honest with your partner about financial matters?
2. Do you believe your partner is honest with you about financial matters?
3. Are you happy with the way your partner spends and saves money?
4. Do you understand the root of your partner's financial attitudes?
5. Is money rarely a source of conflict?
6. If you have arguments about financial issues, do you resolve them quickly and adequately?
7. Are you content with your current financial roles?
8. Do you feel "safe" with the way your partner deals with financial issues?
9. Do you take each other's feelings and needs into consideration when making key financial decisions?
10. Do you feel comfortable revealing financial mistakes to your partner and vice versa?

When you're finished, tally your yes and no responses. The more yes responses you have, the more compatible you and your partner likely are concerning most money issues. If you do have negative reactions to any of the questions, don't worry; now is the perfect time to work with your partner towards overcoming them.

ARE YOU PLAYING FOR THE SAME TEAM?

One of the most effective pieces of advice I have ever received regarding being one-half of a healthy couple came from my best friend's mother: "Always remember that you are two players on the same team." This is a perfect visual. The moment you two begin to duke it out, conjure up the image of a field with two teams staring the other down, oppositional and ready for battle.

Where are you and your partner? Are you side by side, fighting for a common victory, or facing off against each other, ready and eager to knock the other down? If you realize that you are seeing the other person as an opponent when a money issue arises, back up. It's going to do you no good to continue with this mind-set. After advising thousands of couples, I found many to be in bitter rivalry with each other when it comes to money, a situation that was never conducive to an effective or pleasant partnership. By reminding yourself that you are on the same team and fighting for the same common goal, you can kick yourself out of any destructive behavior patterns and work together toward making positive, lasting progress.

GETTING STARTED

First, recognize the importance of addressing differences and similarities that you have with your partner. Money is one of the top three causes of conflict in relationships. Let's face it: it's not just dollars you're talking about when you debate who pays what, why bills don't go out on time, and whether or not to buy the French teak crib. Money goes to the core of our being: what we value, what makes us feel safe, secure, powerful, free, successful, and worthwhile.

"YOU DON'T REALLY KNOW ME, DO YOU?"

Does it ever feel as though you and your partner are completely different? If so, you're in the majority. A recent survey of married couples found that most husbands and wives don't share a completely matching set of financial goals, priorities, and worries.

- More than 8 in 10 of those polled (84%) admit money is a major cause of tension in their marriage.
- Disagreements about sex took a back seat to finances (43% money, 20% sex).
- Financial disputes are more heated and common than those about in-laws (34% money, 24% in-laws).

Fighting about money is so common that it's almost a cliché. The study found that traditional roles concerning money are also a factor: husbands take on most of the long-term financial planning, and wives are in charge of the household's day-to-day finances.

—*Source: MONEY Magazine, April 2007 issue*

If you're like the vast majority of couples, your entire financial situation will change dramatically during pregnancy and immediately after the birth of your child. To understand what this change will likely be and to plan effectively for it, you'll need to engage in healthy, productive, and open communication. In addition, because this will need to be done whenever money matters arise, try to make it as enjoyable and anxiety-free as possible.

There is an old but accurate saying: people don't change; they just become more themselves. What does this mean in the context of money and babies? Entrenched habits usually deepen rather than lessen. Change isn't easy; it requires a great deal of hard work and determination. Compromise is often an essential tool when addressing financial issues. Because of this, if differences in your core money values are making it hard to move forward, this is when you need to work even harder to find a middle ground that both of you can live with.

TALKING AND LISTENING: A DYNAMIC DUO!

Because money is such a major part of our daily lives, it is more than likely that you and your partner are already communicating about it in some way. It's hard to imagine a life together without having to address such questions as, "Should we get new furniture or put it off for a while?" "Have you paid that Visa bill yet?" and "You spent how much on *that*?"

That's talking, but not necessarily solving differences. Remember, now is a critical time to plan for your family's financial future. You're in the middle of making key decisions and purchases, so you may need to take your communication to another level to determine what's best for all of you.

Healthy financial discourse can be a challenge, but it can also be an illuminating, eye-opening experience. In addition to learning more about your partner, you will likely learn a bit about yourself, too. You get to see how the other thinks, what each of you values, where you take risks, and where each pulls back. To know this about yourself and your partner can deepen your relationship on many levels.

Unfortunately, the majority of couples I have worked with have never discussed the subject of money any more deeply than what bills are due or who spent too much this month. Suddenly, with a new baby on the way, there's a whole host of new financial issues to consider. It isn't uncommon for new parents to feel overwhelmed, which then leads to unproductive arguments and compounding problems. With so much at stake, is this the direction you want to take? If your answer is no, then the time is now to discuss what needs to be done and make productive decisions about how to achieve your common goals.

Stay Positive

The advice to stay positive may sound obvious, but you can't start a productive discussion about money when you want to throw the checkbook at your partner's head. When talking about money, you both need to be in a relatively calm and harmonious state of mind. This is not to say you shouldn't be upset if your partner was supposed to pay the mortgage but "forgot," and now the loan is in default. The message is that constructive talk doesn't usually come from a heated beginning—and even if it does, it usually takes a very long time to overcome the anger and start working on constructive solutions. As mentioned before, do you really have that kind of time or energy right now?

When you and your partner are in a good state of mind, start your talk and keep the following things in mind.

Always Begin With the Positive. A little flattery can get you everywhere, and starting a conversation about money on a positive note can generate some wonderful momentum and propel your talk in the right direction. When two people are positive, optimistic, and committed, they are often capable of making real progress and achieving wonderful things.

What do you like about each other's attitudes and behaviors toward money? Do you have a mutual respect and appreciation for each other? There has to be something you can do to start things on a positive note! Stretch if you have to. Keep in mind that everyone wants to feel respected, validated, and appreciated by their loved one. You can't go wrong with a sincere compliment.

Talk Openly About the Issues. To have your discussions about money be productive, you're going to have to address them in an open and honest way. This means talking about all those difficult and challenging issues that we all like to avoid whenever possible. Now is not the time to hide facts or choose to worry about the issues later. Remember, if you approach things in the right way, you can make positive and lasting progress. For example, if your partner is an overspender, you might say that although you like her spontaneity and generosity, you are worried that important financial goals will be neglected unless you both stick to a budget. Think about how you would like someone to approach his criticism of you.

Let Your Feelings and Needs Be Known. Because now is the time to discuss all important money issues, there is no better time to address your desires and needs. How do you feel about income and power within your relationship? This is an especially important topic if one of you is considering becoming a stay-at-home parent and will not be earning a paycheck as usual.

Leaving a job to stay at home with a baby is a huge transition for many individuals. It often puts a lot of pressure on the breadwinner and a lot of guilt on the parent who stays home. Talk about your hopes and fears in this area. Does the person who makes the money, or who makes most of it, have more say in the shopping, savings, and investment decisions? If that is the case, are you both fine with that? Discuss these issues thoroughly.

Be Honest and Expect Honesty. How important is honesty to you? Now how truthful are you about finances? Are you honest with your partner? As a financial counselor, I frequently assisted couples with managing their money so they could get out of debt. I saw firsthand how often couples keep secrets about money. Whether it was a credit card that one partner used without telling the other or hiding missed payments, secrets about debt and money were commonplace.

Why hide financial facts? Many of us want to retain a sense of independence when we partner up. Because you have to do a lot of compromising in a marriage or partnership, an easy way to keep your individuality is to keep money secrets. For others, shame is to blame. There's a tendency to sweep mistakes under the rug rather than confront them. Are you keeping secrets? You can't expect your partner to be honest if you aren't.

Many times during a counseling session, one partner would pull me aside to "confess" her financial sins and be filled with fear and anxiety about what to do next. My advice was to always take the honest approach, from the very beginning if possible, and work together toward overcoming any hurdles.

We all have secrets, but now that you have or are about to have a baby, this is the perfect opportunity to open up about your attitudes and actions concerning money. You want your child to be able to come to you with financial concerns, so you should model this behavior by being honest and open as well.

Being secretive or avoidant can make a bad situation worse. If you went on a spending spree at the mall and exceeded your credit limit, what good could come from hiding the statement when it arrives in the mail? I have seen far too many couples destroyed by keeping money secrets. Many couples consider such deception a form of cheating, a financial infidelity if you will. It changes the dynamics of a relationship and can be hard to overcome. If you lie about a credit card, what else are you holding back?

Be Willing to Compromise. Don't you just hate having to compromise, especially if you're the only one doing it? On that note, isn't it wonderful when your partner eases up and bends a bit? I'm sure you know by now that when you are one half of a couple, you can't always have your way. (Believe me, I've tried.)

Ideally, all of this talk about money issues should be doing two things: giving you and your partner a greater understanding of each other's financial ideas, background, and aspirations as well as getting you working together on making your goals for your family come true.

With each discussion, there should be at least some movement toward a middle ground, with each person making concessions that bring you closer together. Remember to adopt a positive approach to every conversation about money. For some, compromise means everyone loses; for others, it means everyone wins. The former attitude will certainly get you the farthest. Enter into every conversation about money with optimism and be ready and willing to negotiate. If there are some things that you absolutely won't budge on, be prepared to give a reasonable explanation as to why that is. "Because I said so" or "because that's the way I feel" isn't enough.

If you want to avoid hearing "I never said that!" when you know that she definitely said it, try taking notes during particularly contentious discussions. This may sound a bit extreme, even silly, but trust me, you will be thankful later. If you are like many couples, you talk deep into the night, and one of you will agree to something ("Okay, I am happy you are going to be a stay-at-home dad, and I'm willing to work overtime three nights a week to make it work") only to renege later. These notes aren't to be used in a fit of anger if the other person goes back on their word, but they can be helpful to have a record of what you and your partner finally decided. Making sure that both of you say what you mean can be achieved by treating the discussion as seriously as possible.

Commit to What You Say. Notes aside, make every effort to stick to your word. In the interest of saving an otherwise good relationship, you may have to change the way you have been doing things. Change is not easy, it takes effort and commitment. Always remember, that you're working together toward goals that you both decided are best for your family.

Don't Feel Pressured to Do It All at Once. There can be a tendency to tackle every financial issue in one sitting. As previously stated, discussing money isn't always a fun and worry-free experience, so you may feel compelled to race through it to get it over with. This approach can easily backfire. Conversations about money can be a real test of your patience and concentration, and as you go along, you may not be in the right frame of mind to give each issue the amount of focus and attention it deserves. Remember, just like your relationship, everything doesn't happen all at once; things progress and evolve over time. Go slowly. These issues are important, and it's not in your best interest to race through them.

Topics to Discuss: The Biggies

Once you set the stage for an open, honest, and productive talk, know what you are going to need to discuss. There are likely many topics to explore and some key subjects that you will need to come together on. Some will require your immediate attention, and some will impact your lives in the distant future. Regardless, there's a lot of wisdom in discussing your financial concerns now. You don't want an unpleasant shock when the time comes to make a critical financial decision, and learning about how your partner feels will bring you closer together. It's amazing what we assume about our partners, only to find out our preconceived notions couldn't have been farther from the truth.

Sit down and go over what is happening with your money on a regular basis. No one person in the relationship should know how much the phone bill is. Both of you should be aware of the details of the household spending, savings, and investing. Don't just put it in the other person's hands and not think of it. Even if you aren't the active money manager, you should at least know what's going on. In passing conversation, ask how your investments are doing or how much there is in savings right now. Being removed from money is never a good thing. Here are some of the major financial topics to come together on that new parents often face.

Will One of You Be a Stay-at-Home-Parent? Even if you are both on the same page with this subject right now, take the time to discuss it again—and again and again. There are several elements of this issue to explore, and most of the time, there will be a significant financial sacrifice involved with losing an income if both of you were working before baby's arrival.

Who will quit his job to stay at home with baby? Most of the time, the woman quits her job and stays home, but the tide is turning. Today, nearly 200,000 fathers leave work and take on the full time parenting duty. There is no harm in considering all options. In strict economic terms, the person who makes the least amount of money should be the stay-at-home parent, but the issue is by no means so black-and-white. Talk openly with your partner about why you or the other person wants or feels the need to be a stay-at-home parent.

Are you both willing and able to make it work financially? Are you willing to move to a smaller space or make other financial sacrifices over the long term? It's one thing to scrape by for a month or two, quite another to eat noodles for years. Be realistic about how you are going to make it work.

You're going to need to come together on all the life changes this decision will mean for you and your family. Above all, try to be flexible when discussing stay at home parenting and losing income. It can be a heated and intensely emotional issue.

Brainstorm what will happen if it just doesn't turn out the way you planned. It's not uncommon for new parents to be at work and discover it's not for them. They can't focus, and their productivity drops. The truth is that they want to be home with their child. The opposite could hold true as well. After a couple of months, they are exhausted, frazzled, needy for adult interaction, and missing their work environment. They crave their desk. Feelings change. Despite the amount of thought and planning you may have put into your decision, the arrangements you've made with your employer, the hours of conversations you've had with your partner and friends, it may not be quite like you thought when reality kicks in.

Discuss the possibility of change and be prepared if it happens. Nothing is set in stone, and at this point in your life, it is crucial to remain flexible and receptive to the possibility that things might not work out quite as planned. Discussing this now is a much better strategy than letting it blindside you and your partner down the road.

Saving. Some people are natural savers, and some people aren't. There may or may not be one in your household, and if there isn't, then you and your partner are going to have to decide how to plan financially for the future, including whether or not one of you is going to take the reins for the good of the family. No matter who you are, what you do, or how much money you have coming in, you've got to develop a plan for savings. Otherwise, I can almost guarantee that you will spend every dime of what comes in. Money just doesn't fall into a savings account on its own. You and your partner have got to come together about how to put cash away to be prepared for a financial crisis. You should talk about the following:

- Who will open and manage the accounts?
- How much money should be put away, and what the savings schedule should be?
- When and for what reasons can you dip into your savings?

Spending. How large does a purchase have to be before you feel the need to tell your partner about it: a $0.95 pack of gum, a $150 coat, a $500 laptop? This is not necessarily about approval; it is about planning. As a couple with intertwined goals and merged funds, you are in this together. Talk about how you would feel if your partner spent an amount of money that makes you uncomfortable without discussing it with you first. Not doing so can be a relationship killer; I've seen it happen over and over again. Sure, you both want a level of autonomy and the freedom to do what you want without someone looking over your shoulder. Just do so with respect for your partner's feelings and needs.

Again, as you prepare for your baby's arrival, you're going to be spending your cash on items you may have never bought before. One person's splurges are another's standards. Before you go wild, first decide with your partner what needs to be purchased. Then set a dollar figure that you are both fine with and decide how you plan to purchase the items on your list, including what goes on the credit cards and how fast they will be paid off.

MONEY AND MARRIAGE

Available research indicates that nearly three in ten couples have different views regarding money matters. Among married adults ...

- 56 percent say that both they and their spouse always look for ways to save money.
- 6 percent say that both they and their spouse don't try particularly hard to save.
- 30 percent say that they and their spouse have different attitudes about saving. (These are the couples most likely to argue about money.)
- 52 percent of these couples say they often or sometimes disagree about money, compared with 38 percent of all married couples.

—Source: Pew Research Center: We Try Hard. We Fall Short. Americans Assess Their Saving Habits; January 24, 2007

Debt. You may want to have a nice glass of wine or cup of tea before beginning this discussion. Talking about debt can get ugly, but it doesn't have to. You'll need to be completely open and honest with each other to address these very important issues. It's time to lay the cards on the table, so to speak. Attitudes about arrearage vary considerably from person to person—one of you may feel that debt isn't so bad, while it may be completely unacceptable to the other. Know exactly

- how many credit cards you both have;
- what, if any, credit card balances you have, including fees and interest rates and when and how you plan to pay them off;
- whether the accounts are joint or individual;
- the types of purchases that are acceptable to make with the cards; and
- the total amount of debt you have.

Both you and your partner should always be completely aware of the amount of debt that you hold, both individually and as a couple. I cannot stress this enough. If you need to, pull copies of your credit reports, show them to each other, and discuss them. This should not fill you with dread. Approach the issue as an opportunity to recognize any financial problems you may have and take decisive action to fix them.

Money Management. Who is taking care of the bills in your home? Is it the person who has the time and the know-how or the one who always manages to lose the paperwork? Is this an area that you and your partner can handle together, or would it be best to have one of you take charge? All of these questions need to be addressed and as early as possible. An arrangement can work better in theory than actual practice, then be open to the possibility of trying an alternate plan. You can switch off from month to month or every six months. You can sit down and do it as a couple. You can have one do the bills and the other review them for accuracy. Sometimes, it takes trying a few different arrangements before you discover what works best for your family.

Do your best to streamline the money management process. Now is the time to rely on technology to get you though. For example, I can't say enough about automatic bill pay. As soon as you can, take 20 minutes out of your life to set it up with your financial institution's website so all you have to do is click your mouse to pay a bill. It's free and you don't need stamps. Just remember to continue to monitor your account statements.

Decide whether or not you and your partner will be maintaining joint or individual bank accounts. There is no right answer to the question of whether or not couples should merge their bank accounts. What works for some couples may be disastrous for you. Be *practical.* If the account is jointly held, then both of you have equal access to activity; if it is individually held, then only the person who opened it can access it.

In my experience, a joint savings account is a great option for couples, because you are (in theory) just adding to the balance. One account adds up to less paperwork to review, which is always nice. You may also find that opening a savings account together for a specific goal, such as socking away money for a big vacation, can be a really effective and enjoyable way to accumulate desired funds and reach your monetary goals.

The major benefit of a jointly held checking account is that both of you are aware of the money that is being spent. The drawback is that they require a fair amount of communication so neither of you inadvertently overdraws the account. The last thing you want to have happen is for your partner to hit the ATM to withdraw a lot of money and neglect to tell you. If you don't have the time or desire for a lot of discussion about who wrote what check and for what amount, then maybe it's best for you to maintain individual checking accounts. You may not know what your partner is "up to," but that doesn't mean you can't or shouldn't ask.

Long-term Goals. What goals do you want to accomplish with your family's money, not just today but years from now? Talk about them with your partner! You should absolutely set some long-term objectives. Look forward to having this discussion; it can be a fun opportunity to get your hopes and dreams out in the open. Keep the conversation positive and express what you would really like to do with your money. This is not necessarily the discussion about exactly how much it's going to cost to achieve these dreams; rather it's about getting like-minded and excited about all the wonderful opportunities that await your growing family.

If you're a renter now but want to transition into homeownership, or if you own your own home but now need a larger one to make room for your new baby, this is a perfect time to talk about housing issues. That might include discussing the possibility of moving to a different neighborhood, one with better schools, public transportation, access to playgrounds, cultural events, or a place where your child can run around free and safe. We all have our unique dreams for how we will raise our family. Again, now is the time to let your partner know how you feel.

You may be ready to trade in your MINI Cooper for a minivan. (It's pretty hard to fit a baby car seat into the former.) Maybe you now need a second car or one that is safer. Get the automobile section from the newspaper and begin discussing what you would like to have. You are going to want to keep your child safe, and that means a reliable, well-built vehicle. Are you in good financial position for this? Discuss a good strategy for you and your partner to meet your needs.

If you're young parents, it may seem strange to think about, talk, and plan for your retirement now. After all, you've only just begun your life! Nevertheless, as with all investments, the earlier you begin, the more time your savings has to grow. In addition, you may feel a touch more responsible right now than you have in the past. Preparing for retirement, even if you are 22, is a responsible thing to do. Invest well and early, and you may be able to begin your golden years much earlier than if you put it off until later. Talk about when you would love to start that stage of your lives and what you'd like it to be like. Are you traveling the globe, playing golf, or sitting on your porch reading and relaxing? Plan it as a couple.

Not everyone loves to travel, but if you and your partner do, discuss what you want out of vacations. Will they be trips to Disneyland, camping in the great outdoors, or photo safaris in Africa? Do you want one blowout vacation every couple of years or several smaller ones throughout the year? Discuss the potential costs and what each of you feels comfortable spending. Again, plan early for what you want. It's the best way to make your wishes a reality.

Planning for your child's education may be one of your long-term goals. If the two of you are on the same page with what you envision for your child's education, terrific. If you aren't, you'll need to discuss this major expense. Sure, you won't need to have the funds in place for about another 17 years, but because you get the most bang for your buck if you start saving and investing immediately, now is the time to make these decisions together.

Saving for college can be a contentious subject. Certainly your opinion is based on your experiences and values. Maybe one of you did not go to college, or one of you thinks it's unnecessary. Perhaps one of you dreams of sending your child to an ultra-exclusive private university, while the other will be happy with a public school near home. You may believe that a student's job is to be the best, most committed student and that she shouldn't have to work to pay for any of her education, but your partner believes just the opposite. Be prepared for any and all of these scenarios to arise, and be sure to discuss the following:

- Why or why not do you want to pay for college?
- How important is cost when working with your child to pick the right college?

- Would you be okay with paying for some of the expenses: tuition but not board, for example, or tuition and board but not entertainment?
- How do you feel about student loans? Do you believe that it is okay for your child to graduate with debt?

Naturally, when planning for future goals, you're also going to need to work out on an investment strategy. Decide if one of you will take charge of this important task or if both of you will be equally active in these decisions. In either case, discuss the concept of risk versus reward. Tell each other what you are comfortable with. Some people hyperventilate at the possibility of losing a penny, while others can't abide by the slow and steady approach. My advice is this: *both* of you should be equally knowledgeable about investments. There are countless resources on the subject, but my favorite tool is Investopedia.com. This website contains a wealth of valuable information (pun very much intended).

In short, take the time to talk to your partner about money issues with patience and respect. Acknowledge and accept your differences and openly appreciate the changes each of you makes for your family. You are in this together. If the discussion gets too hot, step back for a while; too often, couples approach their personal economic matters with grim determination, which isn't fun for anyone.

If you suspect that there are deeper issues at play and that you cannot resolve differences or find peace with your money matters, don't hesitate to seek counseling. Unresolved money issues can drive a terrible, sometimes permanent, wedge between two people who truly do love each other. Don't let this happen. Your baby depends on you both, and your family unit will operate much more efficiently, and happily, if you work together as a team.

CHAPTER SUMMARY

- Recognize that you and your partner are both in this equally, even if one of you works and the other stays home.
- Understand and address differences and similarities that you have with your partner.

- Do not allow differences about money to go unaddressed, they will only get worse.
- Make a conscious effort to be a better communicator, both in talking and listening.
- When discussing financial matters, be positive, open, and honest.
- Discuss the important topics early: stay-at-home parenting, saving, investing, spending, debt, and goals.
- Be ready and willing to compromise.
- Don't make promises you can't keep.
- Get professional financial help if necessary.

Chapter 8

On Your Own

Single Solutions

THE VAST MAJORITY OF money matters are equally relevant for single- and dual-parent families. To achieve economic empowerment, we all need to pay attention to our spending and charging habits, refine them if necessary, and plan for the future. However, single parents also need to tackle some unique financial concerns to achieve financial stability and happiness for their family.

Some single parents are swimming in cash and without a monetary care in the world. Unfortunately, more often than not, this isn't the case. The fact is, single parents typically have greater and more complicated economic needs than those who are part of a couple.

So many single parents I have worked with expressed that they often feel alone, which of course isn't true. Today there are approximately 14 million single mothers and fathers in America. In fact, approximately 40 percent of all children today are born into one-parent families.

Roughly half of all marriages end in divorce, so even children born into two-parent families may end up in a one-parent situation at some point in their lives. Therefore, while you may indeed be solo, you are most surely not alone. Furthermore, you *can* make single parenthood work by knowing which financial issues you have to contend with and then facing each one head-on, armed with accurate information and a positive attitude.

The special concerns for single parents often begin with child (and sometimes spousal) support. Even if you are entitled to receive this money, the amount can be inadequate to cover all of your bills, and collecting may be no simple endeavor. If you have gone through a divorce or custody battle, chances are you have hefty legal fees to pay, which can heighten the stress of trying to meet the financial needs of you and your new baby.

Employment is likely a requirement rather than an option, and no matter how much you may adore your job, finding a comfortable balance between being the primary breadwinner and being the parent you dream of can be a challenge. In addition, securing excellent, affordable child care often takes on greater importance for single parents than double-parent families. On top of all this, trying to manage your money effectively while coping with everything else going on may feel overwhelming. Tasks like monitoring checking account statements and paying bills requires setting aside the time to do it, and time is the one thing that single parents often have in very short supply. However, although single parenthood often requires a bit more effort and dedication, success and happiness are certainly achievable goals.

No less vital for single parents is the emotional aspect of being the sole caregiver. A healthy outlook and mind-set is crucial to addressing financial issues. I can't tell you how many single parents I have worked with who've been caught in the trap of buying things for their child out of guilt. They often think, "Perhaps a new toy will reduce the pain of not being there as often as I wish I could." This thought process often leads to overspending and debt, triggering serious financial and emotional stress.

Essentially, as a single parent, you have a lot on your plate. It can be difficult to find the resources to take care of a new baby while

SINGLE PARENTS ACROSS AMERICA

Most are mothers:
- 83.1% of custodial parents are mothers.
- 16.9% of custodial parents are fathers.

Of the mothers who are custodial parents …
- 45.9% are currently divorced or separated.
- 30.5% have never been married.
- 21.0% are married. (In most cases, these numbers represent women who have remarried.)
- 1.7% were widowed.

Of the fathers who are custodial parents …
- 56.4% are divorced or separated.
- 23.1% are currently married. (In most cases, these numbers represent men who have remarried.)
- 19.7% have never married.
- 0.8% were widowed.

A good portion of the mothers are not "young":
- 36.8% of custodial mothers are 40 or older.

Most are raising one child:
- 55.6% of custodial mothers are raising one child.
- 44.4% have two or more children living with them.

Most are employed:
- 80% of custodial single mothers are gainfully employed:
  - 50.5% work full-time, year-round.
  - 29.6% work part-time or seasonally.
- 89.8% of custodial single fathers are gainfully employed:
  - 70.6% work full-time, year-round.
  - 9.2% work part-time or seasonally.

Most do not live in poverty:
- 26.1% of custodial single mothers and their children live in poverty.
- 13.4% of custodial single fathers and their children live in poverty.

(continued)

SINGLE PARENTS ACROSS AMERICA (continued)

Most do not receive public assistance:

- 30.3% of all single parents receive public assistance.
- Only 8.4% of single parents receive Temporary Assistance for Needy Families (TANF).

—*Source: Custodial Mothers and Fathers and Their Child Support: 2003, released by the U.S. Census Bureau in July 2006.*

---

simultaneously enjoying life as a parent. Thankfully, a lot of these issues can be dealt with early, *before* things get out of control. You *can* make single parenthood work by recognizing what you need to do and taking the necessary steps to make it happen now.

SINGLE PARENT ISSUES

As previously stated, single parents face a variety of unique issues. Here are some of the primary money-related concerns that you will likely need to face—and how to overcome them.

Child Support

Based on my years of financial consulting experience, child support can be one of the most contentious issues that single parents have to contend with. Those who are entitled to it sometimes do not pursue it, those who are paying often grumble about the cost, and those who are supposed to pay but do not are furious about their ruined credit and the other highly unpleasant repercussions of being a "deadbeat" parent. Both sides couldn't be more passionate about their being "right."

The fact is that single parents who do not receive monetary support for their child often struggle needlessly. It's heartbreaking to hear the stories of parents trying desperately to make ends meet on one income. Even when they do get support, sometimes the amount is insufficient to meet even basic needs. The primary reason for this is that raising children in two households is far more expensive than doing it in one.

Although both mothers and fathers who do not live together struggle with financial problems, almost across the board, the parent who has primary custody shoulders the majority of the financial responsibility. Child support, for the 45 percent of custodial parents who receive the full amount, is sometimes too low for comfort.

If your baby was or will be born outside of marriage, the other parent, if he or she is not in the picture, is still responsible for making child support payments. The same goes if you are awarded sole legal or physical custody of your baby as a result of divorce.

Before pursuing child support, it is a good idea to know how the courts determine the sum you may get. While this is mainly the realm of lawyers and the courts, it's vital for everyone in this position to be armed with some basic information in a few key areas of the law.

Each state has developed its own guidelines to determine appropriate child support payments, so depending on what state you live in, the payments you receive can vary widely. In some parts of the country, the guidelines are extremely strict, so judges don't have a lot of flexibility when making their order; in others, the judge gets to use much discretion based on the facts of the individual case. In general, most states look at some fundamental factors when coming up with a monthly payment:

- Your child's specific economic needs, including health insurance, child care, education, and so on
- Your income and assets and the other parent's income and assets
- Your child's standard of living before divorce or separation

The last point is an effort to ensure that your child, if he will be moving between the households of the custodial and noncustodial parent, doesn't have a huge difference in lifestyle. In some cases, the court may order that some of the money awarded is to be spent on equalizing the standard of living in one of the homes.

Two key factors for calculating child support are the percentage of time the parent has the children and the income of both parents. To get a pretty good idea of what you may be entitled to receive, visit the

U.S. Department of Health and Human Services: Administration for Children and Families/Office of Child Support Enforcement website, *www.acf.hhs.gov*, for a state-by-state child support calculator.

A crucial expense that single parents should prepare for, and not skimp on, is good legal counsel. I strongly recommend that you do not try to do this on your own and never agree to settle on a custody or support arrangement without consulting a lawyer. Doing so could have severe and permanent repercussions. Inequity abounds, and there have been cases where the parent who could least afford to pay support ends up with nothing or having to pay the other person. I've seen it happen.

Sure, both parents should be accountable for their child's financial welfare, but unfortunately, many parents shirk this duty. If this is the case for you, then you'll have to be the one who takes action to collect what you are entitled to. Although this can take a lot of effort, remember that the money isn't just for you; it's so you can properly care for your baby. In case you're wondering, you don't have to pay taxes on the money you receive for child support.

Too many single parents forgo child support. The reasons vary, but in my experience the most common reasons are not wanting to have anything to do with the other person for personal motives (i.e., "I hate him and never want to hear his name or see his face again!") and not having the time, money, or energy for the battle. These rationales are valid. While I would never advocate having a relationship with someone you think will do you or your baby harm, I do believe that fighting for financial support is almost always worth the effort because—I'll say it again—in most cases, raising a child on your own with one income is just too hard.

To get what's due, you may have to go to court and duke it out. Making arrangements outside of the court system is sometimes done (it is nice to be amicable), but after hearing countless stories of situations that started off friendly but ended up contentious, I highly recommend taking the legal route from the start. You should hire a lawyer, which can be another big expense, but if you can get the other person to pay support for the next 18 years or more of your child's life, it is a sensible investment.

Keep in mind that if the other person doesn't shell out what they are supposed to, the consequences are quite severe. Wage garnishments, liens, seizure of property, revocation of licenses, income tax interceptions, public humiliation, and even jail are among the repercussions. Contact your state district attorney's office for more information about allowable collection and punitive methods in your area:

- National Association of Attorneys General (NAAG)
  2030 M Street NW, 8th Floor
  Washington, DC 20036
  (202) 326-6000
  www.naag.org

Divorce and Separation Issues

If you're going through a divorce or separation right now, you know that it can be a long and painful process, and one that can have a significant impact on your ability to focus on key parenting issues. In an effort to help you move forward and allow you to concentrate on taking care of your child, there are a few key items you should consider.

Pull Copies of Your Credit Report. We all have secrets, but if you want to know what kind of financial dealings your partner has been up to, at least in the borrowing arena, pull copies of your credit report from the moment you know divorce is in your future.

Although credit reports are not merged for married couples, they do list all of your, and any jointly held, credit-related activity. You may very well discover accounts or debts that you weren't aware of. Simply put, you need to know what you're dealing with because you may be responsible for some of the debt even if you had no idea of its existence.

Close Jointly Held Accounts. If you have credit accounts that you opened together, now is the time to close them. If the other partner uses the accounts before the divorce or legal separation, you may be held responsible for repayment. When you cancel the accounts, make a request to the creditor that they read "closed by consumer," a notation that reflects more positively on your credit report than if it reads "closed by creditor."

You may also ask the financial institution if you can change the title from joint to individual. If you do the latter, make sure the beneficiaries (the person whom you want to inherit the account's funds) reflect your current wishes. Chances are that the last thing you want is for your assets to go to your ex, but people forget—it happens all the time.

Open Accounts in Your Name. If you never had financial accounts in your name, visit your bank or credit union and do so immediately. Open a checking, savings, and credit account. This way you will be able to launch your economic independence, something you will need in the next stage of your life.

A credit card can be hard to open if you have no established credit history. If that's the case, consider a secured credit card. Almost all financial institutions offer them. To open one, all you need to do is put down a set amount of money, usually a few hundred dollars. That amount will be your credit limit. Use the card responsibly on a regular basis, and you are on your way to creating a great credit history. After a year or so of using the card, you may be able to transfer it to an unsecured account and get your security deposit back, which you can immediately put into a savings account!

Know Your State's Community and Separate Property Laws. Each state has different laws regarding debt and divorce. If you live in a community property state, any debt you or your spouse incurred during the marriage, regardless of who racked it up, is a marital debt, meaning the creditor can hold both of you liable for repayment. In a separate property state, this may not be the case. Many newly single parents are horrified to learn that they'll be responsible for their ex's financial indiscretions. There is nothing like finding out your former spouse spent a few thousand dollars on something and that you're stuck with at least part of the bill.

As of this writing, there are nine community property states: Arizona, California, Idaho, Louisiana, Nevada, New Mexico, Texas, Washington, and Wisconsin. In Alaska, couples have the option to adopt community property rules when they marry.

Postdivorce Debt. Keep in mind that a divorce decree (a court-imposed arrangement where each of you agrees to pay specific debt) is for convenience and peace only. If the account is jointly held, creditors can come after either of you to collect what is owed no matter who is supposed to pay. That is why it's important for both parties to treat the postdivorce debts responsibly. Missed payments affect each of your credit reports, and collection action may start for either of you. You can't really control what the other person does, but it is good to be aware of what *could* happen.

Divorce, Debt, and Bankruptcy. If you suspect that your spouse will file for bankruptcy after the divorce, be sure to discuss this possibility with your lawyer before you go to court. The separation agreement may be structured to take bankruptcy into consideration. If your former spouse does discharge joint debts in bankruptcy, you may be held responsible for the entire payment, though sometimes bankruptcy court will discharge or release the spouse from paying those debts.

Alimony and Spousal Support. Along with child support payments, you may also be entitled to alimony, or spousal support. There are two basic types: temporary, which is designed to allow the recipient enough time to get back on his financial feet, and permanent. As with child support, the amount you may get is dependent on the state you reside in. It almost always factors in how you and your ex lived during the marriage. The court also looks at the following:

- The incomes, expenses, earning capacities, debts, and assets of both of you
- How long you were married
- If you are looking after dependant children, and if working will interfere with that duty
- The age and health of both of you
- The amount of time it can conceivably take for you, as the person receiving support, to re-enter the workforce

If you do receive spousal support payments, be aware that your ex will be able to deduct the payments on his taxes. In addition, the amount you receive is considered income, so you will have to pay taxes on the support.

Divorce is one of the top three reasons people declare bankruptcy (the others being medical problems and unemployment or underemployment). It can be so emotionally stressful that the last thing you may feel like doing is spending time and energy on your money issues. However, you have a baby to think about,

> **SINGLE PARENTS SPEND MORE**
>
> Those who earn more than $40,000 will spend about 32 percent of their income each year on a child, while two-parent households earning the same income will spend just 23 percent of their earnings on their child.
>
> —*U.S. Census Bureau, 2003*

and you've got to be practical. If you need to, get professional assistance during this time, and not just from your lawyer. Many financial planners specialize in divorce issues. A great resource for further information is the Financial Planning Association, an organization that can provide you with a good referral:

- Financial Planning Association
  600 K Street NW, Suite 201
  Washington, DC 20006
  800-322-4237
  www.fpanet.org

A terrific resource for legal guidance and information that is written in layperson's language is Nolo Press, which has a helpful website and series of guidebooks. They publish a comprehensive, state-by-state lawyer directory as well. Go to *www.nolopress.org* for additional information.

Increased Costs for Single Parents

Insurance expenses are especially important for single parents to consider. To protect yourself and your growing family, working the cost of insurance coverage into your budget should be a top priority. All mothers and fathers need to prepare for their families' futures, but single parents sometimes have to go the extra mile.

Life Insurance. One of the most difficult aspects of being the sole provider for your new baby is that she may only have you to rely on. If something happens to you, what will happen to your child? For single parents, life insurance coverage may be the sole means of financial support for their children. To protect your child's future, life insurance is a must. Right now, nearly four in ten single parents have no life insurance coverage of any kind. Among those who have coverage, nearly two-thirds consider their coverage inadequate. Often, there's good reason for this: the typical two-parent household has $250,000 in life insurance coverage compared to just $60,000 for its single-parent counterpart. While $60,000 may sound like a lot of money, it costs a lot more than that to raise a child today. Chapter 11, "Making It Happen," will delve into the various types of life insurance products in more detail.

Health Coverage. When the financial burden is on you alone, making sure you have enough medical coverage is even more important than for two-parent families. If you have insurance, consider adding to it; you certainly don't want to cut corners where the health of your baby is concerned. If you don't have a disability policy through work, consider getting one.

When my daughter was four years old, she came down with a stomach illness that kept her in the hospital for about five days. During our stay, I noticed a baby in another room, a little girl of about 18 months. Not once did I see a parent with her. Eventually, I found out that the baby had to have heart surgery, but unfortunately the mother was a single parent who had to work. The operation and hospital stay was going to cost a fortune, and there were other bills that absolutely had to be paid. Apparently, the mother was near hysterics whenever she left her daughter, but if she didn't go, she'd lose her job and wouldn't be able to meet her expenses.

I can't imagine how painful it must have been for her not to be there. To this day, I think about that baby and what her mother must have gone through. As a single parent, you've got to do all that you can do now to prepare your finances so in an emergency you can be there. That may mean making a few more sacrifices than double-parent families have to—saving more, getting better insurance, securing a higher paying job, or reducing expenses. However, the sooner you start, the better off you'll be.

Emergency Savings. Although saving for the inevitable financial crisis is part of every family's good money management, as a single parent, having emergency cash reserves takes on even greater importance. If you can't work, or if you have to pay for an unexpected expense, who are you going to count on to get you through? Most likely, it will be all on your shoulders. This is a major responsibility, so I strongly recommend saving aggressively now with an aim to set aside a reserve of at least six months' worth of necessary expenses.

Child Care. If you are, or will be, receiving child support payments, then some of it will probably be used to pay for child care while you go to work, but what about those times when you might just want to go out for the evening? When there are two of you, the other parent can stay and take care of the baby, but when you're on your own, you very well may have to pay for a sitter. Because the cost for this expense can be high, you may want to begin networking in your neighborhood for other parents who are in similar situations. You may be able to trade care, where you look after the other's child for a night and then he returns the favor. If not, consider factoring the cost of a sitter into your budget.

Housing. Housing costs can be a big stressor for single parents. More often than not, it's just more expensive to raise a child in two homes than in one. After all, if there were two of you living together, you'd be sharing the rent or mortgage, but as a single parent you pay the entire sum. It can be tough to make this expense work, so if you need to, consider utilizing some resources that may be available. An excellent nonprofit organization that can help is CoAbode. They offer a variety of helpful services, but their primary program is Single Mothers House Sharing. It is for mothers (As of this writing there isn't a similar agency for single fathers) who would like to reduce housing costs by pairing up with others in a similar situation.

- CoAbode
  1223 Wilshire Blvd, Suite 102
  Santa Monica, CA 90403
  www.coabode.com

Time. Time has a lot to do with money! As a new parent, you'll find that there may not be enough hours in the day to do everything you need. That includes working so you can take care of your little one in the manner you would like and addressing all pertinent financial matters to better your situation.

Therefore, it pays to network and seek out available resources for assistance. One of the best organizations out there for single parents is Parents Without Partners, Inc. This large, international, nonprofit membership organization is devoted to the welfare and interests of single parents and their children. There are about 200 chapters across the country. Although it's primarily a social networking organization, most chapters also offer lectures by psychologists, lawyers, and other professionals; study groups; training seminars; and leadership and personal growth opportunities. Contact it directly for additional information:

- Parents Without Partners, Inc.
  1650 South Dixie Highway, Suite 510
  Boca Raton, FL 33432
  800-637-7974
  www.parentswithoutpartners.org

THE UPSIDE TO BEING ON YOUR OWN

Considering all the issues you may face, being a single parent may sound a bit daunting. However, always keep in mind that there are some advantages to going at it on your own. Have you heard the way some couples bicker over financial issues? In your own house, you never have to compromise; what you say goes. That autonomy really is pretty amazing and liberating.

In addition, there are a few tax benefits to being a single parent. If you can file as head of household, you will usually pay less in taxes than your married counterparts. You'll also be able to take advantage of a more generous tax bracket and a larger standard deduction. In 2007, the standard deductions were as follows (each year the deductions increase, so contact the Internal Revenue Service for current tax information):

2007 Standard Deduction

Single:	$5,350
Head of Household:	$7,850
Married Filing Jointly:	$10,700
Married Filing Separately:	$5,350
Qualifying Widow/Widower:	$10,700

Make sure you file under the right status. If you file as a single tax-payer by mistake, you'll lose out on the deduction that you are actually due. To qualify for "head of household" status, you need to be unmarried on the last day of the year, provide more than 50 percent of the funds needed to maintain your household, and have your baby living with you for more than half the year. You also have to be a U.S. citizen or a resident alien during the entire tax year. Only one parent can claim each child as a dependent for tax purposes, so if you share equal custody, the two of you are going to have to determine which parent will claim the dependent exemption.

All in all, being a single parent typically means that you have a few more financial responsibilities than someone who has a partner who can take up some of the burden. With a steadfast approach, support from your friends and community, and—most importantly—a belief in yourself, you can pave the way for a secure life for your family and feel incredibly proud about your choices and actions. As always, a little planning goes a long way.

CHAPTER SUMMARY

- Don't buy out of guilt—it's a trap many single parents fall into.
- Make time for money management. Time will be precious, but overdue accounts are too costly to accept.
- Pursue the child support you are due:
  - o Know how it is calculated and what you may be entitled to.
  - o Understand the collection methods that are available.

- Deal with divorce and money issues as soon as possible—close joint accounts and open new ones in your name.
- Know if you are in a community property state and what that means as far as your debts are concerned.
- Understand alimony and pursue it if you are due.
- Prepare for key costs: life insurance, health coverage, emergency savings, child care, and housing.
- Get support via organizations for single parents.
- Take advantage of the independence, autonomy, and tax benefits of being a single parent.

Chapter 9

Working It Out

Employment Issues

A S MARVELOUS AS PARENTHOOD is, there are times when it can feel like a constant struggle between need and desire. One of the most serious of these conflicts concerns work. Certainly you've got to have money coming in to take care of your growing family, but how are you going to do it? Will one of you remain employed while the other stays home (assuming another parent is available to take this on)? If one of you does stop working, how long will it be for—three months, a year, until your child graduates from high school? Will living on one income lead to financial ruin; will returning to work make you a "bad" parent? Don't let these questions keep you up at night—you'll need your sleep to deal with and enjoy your newborn! This chapter will help you make the right decisions about work for you and your family.

WHO GOES BACK TO WORK AND WHEN?

Thanks to the Family Medical Leave Act, if you work for a company with 50 or more employees, you can take 12 weeks of unpaid leave to take care of your newborn baby. However, what happens if your company has fewer employees? You may be back at work before you'd like or sooner than is conducive to being productive on the job. In fact, many women go back to work still experiencing delivery-related symptoms or symptoms associated with the demands of caring for a newborn:

- 76 percent of working mothers return to work within a year after the birth of their children.
- 41 percent of working mothers are back within three months.
- Nearly one in six is back within the first month after delivery.

—*Source: Study of working mothers conducted by the School of Public Health at the University of Minnesota, Family Medicine, March/April 2006.*

STAY-AT-HOME PARENT (SAHP) FINANCIALS

Let's see how you can make it on one income. There are a number of ways to help you figure it all out.

Give It a Quick Calculation

To determine if having you or your partner stay at home makes sound financial sense, make a list of work-related expenses, including the cost of child care, and then subtract them from the income that will be given up. If you come out ahead, is it by a compelling amount? If you are sitting on the fence with what you want to do as far as working or quitting, just seeing the numbers in black and white can give you a push in the right direction.

Determining how losing an income will affect your finances takes some simple calculations. Consider the following example.

Genevieve and her husband Paul earn the same income. They both take home a monthly net paycheck of $2,200. A full-time nanny, the only child care option they are comfortable with, would be $1,800 per month in their area. The difference for one of them to quit, let's say it was Genevieve, would be $400 ($2,200 − $1,800 = $400). However, because she is contributing to her retirement plan, and her employer is matching her savings to the tune of $120 per month, she is losing out on that money as well. Now the cost for her to quit is $520 ($400 + $120 = $520).

After Genevieve adds up all of her work-related costs, gas for commuting, her professional attire and dry cleaning costs, lunches, coffees, and snacks, she finds they total $375 per month. Therefore, if Genevieve were to remain at her job, she would be losing $145 ($520 − $375 − $145) per month.

When both Genevieve and Paul work, their combined income pushes them into a high tax bracket. If she drops her job, their earnings will be taxed at a reduced rate. However, while Genevieve may not be driving as much as she had been, she'll still be using the car and going out for the occasional daytime meal.

The questions are clear: Can Genevieve and Paul *afford* to lose out on $145 per month? What are the full costs of doing so? Are they in a financial position where this amount is required to make ends meet? Will they be able to save for their short- and long-term goals, such as college funding, retirement planning, and vacations? Can they cut down their expenses to make it all work? Even if they're living paycheck to paycheck before the reduction, maybe they can downsize, perhaps lose one of the cars or move into a less expensive home? Only they know what they are comfortable and capable of doing. Just as only you are.

Work Out the Numbers

Will your or your partner's being a SAHP work for your family? Consider the following list of typical work-related expenses (Figure 9.1). For whichever partner is considering becoming a SAHP, mark off the applicable work-related expenses and note what each costs on a monthly basis. Some will likely increase; others will likely decrease. Complete the following work versus home expense worksheet. Estimate any expense increases and decreases, then find the total for each column to see where you stand financially.

Do you come out ahead or behind if you work? Is the difference enough to sway you in either direction? Sometimes, the answer is really

Figure 9.1 *Work Versus Home Expense Worksheet*

WORK VERSUS HOME EXPENSE WORKSHEET			
Expense	**Working**	**Not Working**	**$ Difference**
Child care			
Commuting: tolls, parking, gasoline			
Car insurance			
Clothing expenses			
Gift and entertaining Expenses			
Food: groceries, coffees, snacks, lunches out			
Housekeeping help			
Personal grooming: hair, nails, etc.			
Other			
Other			
Total Expenses (Working):			
Total Expenses (Not Working):			
Total Difference:			

obvious: if child care is going to be as much or more of an expense than what one of you is earning, then financially speaking, it makes sense to quit. Conversely, if losing an income will mean that you won't be able to make ends meet, two incomes makes sense.

Now look at your tax situation. Do two salaries put you in a higher tax bracket? In basic terms, the more you make, the higher your tax rate will be. Figure 9.2 lists federal personal income tax rates for 2006.

Let's say you made a combined income of $95,000 during 2006 and filed "married filing separately." According to the table, the top tax rate for you would be 33 percent. However, if one of you dropped a $45,000-a-year job, your total income would be $50,000, which would place you in the 25 percent tax bracket. That is a big difference.

Figure 9.2 *Federal Personal Income Tax Rate Chart*

2006 FEDERAL PERSONAL INCOME TAX RATES				
Tax Rate	Single Filers	Married Filing Jointly or Qualifying Widow/ Widower	Married Filing Separately	Head of Household
10%	Up to $7,550	Up to $15,100	Up to $7,550	Up to $10,750
15%	$7,551– $30,650	$15,101– $61,300	$7,551– $30,650	$10,751– $41,050
25%	$30,651– $74,200	$61,301– $123,700	$30,651– $61,850	$41,051– $106,000
28%	$74,201– $154,800	$123,701– $188,450	$61,851– $94,225	$106,001– $171,650
33%	$154,801– $336,550	$188,451– $336,550	$94,226– $168,275	$171,651– $336,550
35%	$336,551 or more	$336,551 or more	$168,276 or more	$336,551 or more

I highly recommend using online calculators for accuracy, speed, and ease of use. They allow you to plug in your data to gain a fairly accurate financial estimate. An excellent one to help you determine whether or not shifting from two incomes to one is a sound economic decision can be found at *www.kiplinger.com/tools/managing/afford.html*.

If you decide to go the SAHP route and the income reduction is going to leave you with less money each month, it's time to start looking at where you are spending your money. Figure out where you can make some changes. Start thinking about how you're spending your money right now and what wouldn't be so hard to give up or at least reduce.

Take It for a Test Run
Determining if you can live happily on one income, and in the black rather than the red, requires a bit of time and foresight. Planning works best if you are only a few months into your pregnancy, so again, start early.

First, work with your partner to identify who will be the stay-at-home parent. It usually makes the best economic sense for the person earning the highest paycheck to continue working. During your trial run, the SAHP remains working and deposits every dollar of that paycheck into a separate savings account. Do not use a penny of that income for any living expenses at all during this time frame. Because no month is identical in terms of expenses, this test run should be done for at least three months, but six is better.

There are several benefits to this exercise. First, it won't take long before you really get a feel for what it will be like to live on one person's earnings. While it may not be perfectly accurate, because during this time you are still incurring work-related costs, it will provide you with a good sense of what it's like to drop a paycheck. Another benefit is that during the months of your experiment, you'll have saved a tidy sum for goals, future expenses, or emergency reserves.

TWO-INCOME FAMILY OPTIONS

If having you or your partner quit working outside the home entirely is not going to work because you want that paycheck coming in, weigh other options. Get creative and think about whatever you can do to keep the necessary cash flowing into your household. If you like your job and want to stay with the company you currently work for, consider the possibility of altering your work schedule. Depending on your position and your company's policy, you may be able to maneuver your current position into something that suits all of your needs.

Part-Time Employment
Does it really have to be all or nothing? Many parents are able to have the best of both worlds with one partner working part-time. Is this possible for you? Contact your company's human resources department and find out. You may be able to keep all or some of your benefits if you work a certain number of hours. Many companies require you to work at least 20 hours to maintain benefits. Of course, if you do work part-time, you're still going to have to make arrangements for your baby's care. Will a member of your family do this for free, or will you have to pay someone?

Does this offset the amount of money that part-time employment will provide? Again, consider all variables before making a decision.

Flexible Schedule

Is your employer open to your coming in a bit later in the day, or possibly working weekends rather than weekdays? Perhaps you can work four ten-hour days to secure a full three days off. You won't know until you ask. Depending on the type of work that you do, a flexible schedule may be available to you. Working with your employer to arrange a schedule that allows you to handle all of your responsibilities, while providing you with enough time to care for your child, may be the perfect solution for all involved.

Alternate Work Schedules

Can one of you work a day job and the other the night shift? Perhaps one of you works Monday through Friday, and the other works on the weekends? If paying for day care is not a financially realistic option, and you don't mind spending less time with your partner right now for the sake of the baby and maintaining an adequate combined income, this type of schedule may be just the ticket.

Telecommuting

For some parents, working as a remote employee is ideal. Keep in mind, this does not always mean that you won't need to hire someone to care for your child! Not only is it very difficult to do your job while breast-feeding or holding your baby, most employers expect you to arrange for child care. This means arranging for a nanny, mother's helper, babysitter, or a friend or family member to be there while you perform your job duties. The advantage of telecommuting and working from home is that you won't have to spend time getting ready for your job and commuting and you can spend your breaks and meals with your baby. The downside is that it can really be tempting to dash over to your baby while working when you hear his cries or giggles, which can impact your productivity. One remote employee I know believes that her baby often senses her presence in the home, and when he does, he crawls over to the room where she's working and cries outside the door. This is just a touch distracting!

Job Share

Maybe part-time work in the traditional sense won't be an option at your company or organization because your job requires a full-time employee. If that's the case, maybe they're willing to let you set up a job-sharing arrangement. This is where two employees literally share the same position. Perhaps you will work Monday, Thursday, and half of Friday, and the other person will work Tuesday, Wednesday, and the other half of the Friday shift. Again, although this may not meet your employer's needs, it doesn't hurt to ask, and you may be pleasantly surprised by your employer's flexibility, especially if you've been a valuable employee thus far.

The good news is that more and more companies are recognizing the value of helping their employees balance their work and family life. For example, the vast majority of JetBlue's employees are women in their 30s who are working part-time shifts. Employees have paired up into share-care arrangements to watch each other's kids while another employee is on the phones. JetBlue's one rule is that the kids cannot be heard over the customer service lines.

A growing number of companies are finding that becoming more flexible and creative in an effort to meet the needs of new mothers and fathers is in their best interests. An office-based call center in the United States can expect to lose around 65 percent of its employees a year as a result of the need to care for newborn babies. However, JetBlue's call center maintains 96.5 percent of its employees every year, a figure that indicates a happy and productive staff. That's pretty amazing.

Alternative Employment Options

Perhaps you don't want to or cannot stay with your old job but still need to earn money to meet your expenses? Consider these options.

Consulting/Freelance. While in most cases, pregnancy and new parenthood is not the ideal time to start your own business, it may be something you are willing and able to work toward. Some fields, such as the technology sector, are particularly receptive to independent freelance employees and consultants.

Becoming a consultant, an independent specialist where you come in on a per project basis, can be a good choice for someone seeking to strike a balance between work and home life. As a consultant, you can often set your own hours and don't have to adhere to a strict work schedule.

You may want to consider doing freelance work. This would include such tasks as writing articles for a website or bookkeeping. If you'll be doing either from home, know that it is really hard to get much done while caring for your baby. Most parents of infants find they can get some tasks done while the baby is sleeping, but that is pretty much it. If you want to stay home and earn a living, seriously consider hiring a helper. You will still be there, and there is a cost, but if you try to do both at once, chances are you'll do both poorly and you'll just wind up frustrated and exhausted.

If you are interested in starting your own business as a consultant or freelancer, contact your local Small Business Administration. You will find plenty of educational materials, workshops, and even loans if you need them. In addition, scanning local and online employment classified ads on a regular basis can be a good strategy; they often list available freelance opportunities.

- U.S. Small Business Administration
  SBA Answer Desk
  800-U-ASK-SBA (827-5722)
  www.sba.gov

Opportunities in Child Care. If you love children, starting your own child care business may fit your income needs and lifestyle requirements perfectly. There are several ways you can go about doing this:

- You can be a nanny. Some parents find this appealing because their child will have a play partner.
- You can babysit on an on-call basis. If you don't need regular income and the other family/families don't mind your baby tagging along, this can be a great way to earn some extra cash.
- Start your own day care business. You've got to love all children (not just your own), possess good business acumen, have the right space, and obtain a license and other

credentials. Oh, and you'll need a lot of energy. If this
sounds right for you, running your own day care can be
a great option.

Tutoring. Do you have a special knowledge or skill that you can teach to
someone else? Perhaps you play the piano and can give lessons. Maybe
you're especially good at math or English and can tutor high school students for their exams. Think about what you know that others may pay to
learn. Once you decide what that is, start selling yourself. You can often
advertise your services on community listing or online message boards,
print up flyers and post them around the neighborhood, or just market
your services through word of mouth.

Animal Care. Do you love animals? Consider caring for them as a part-
time business. There are virtually no start-up costs, and the money can
be excellent. Is it possible to take dogs for walks while carrying your
baby in a sling or front carrier? Another option is to feed and look after
your neighbors' pets while they are out of town. If caring for animals
sounds appealing, then get the word out that you're available. If you
are good and reliable, it won't be long before you can build a steady
clientele and add a few hundred dollars to your monthly budget with
just a few hours' work a day.

Make Your Computer Work for You. Editing, copywriting (or any writing), selling things on an online auction, blogging, designing websites,
updating websites, and technical support are just some of the virtually
endless possibilities for what you can do at your computer to make some
extra money. There are all sorts of job board listings for you to check out,
with one of the best being Craigslist: *www.craigslist.org*. Just turn on your
computer, do a little careful research, and get started.

Sales. Are you a persuasive go-getter who's usually able to convince others to see things your way? If so, then sales can be a potentially lucrative
field. There are many products you can sell right out of your home, from
beauty products, such as Avon and Mary Kay, to candles, lingerie, and
more. You may be able to bring your baby with you as you go on sales

calls or throw "sales parties." Do a little research and choose a product that you think you'll be good at selling.

Property Management. Are you handy with tools and are a real people person? If so, then look into becoming a property manager. If you are willing and able to move into a building where you are paid to be there and take care of clogged drains or any other rental issues, this can be a good way for you to stay home rent-free and earn a monthly income. Just be sure that you're capable of handling the sorts of issues and emergencies that may (and often do) arise.

Make, Buy, and/or Sell Things. If you have a creative flair or artistic talent, consider using it to your economic advantage. Your creative niche may include knitting, painting, jewelry making, sewing, calligraphy, or something entire new and unique. I know a prolific and extremely talented artist who whips out beautiful little paintings relatively quickly and sells them on her own website. Once she has the inventory, she sends out an email to her huge network of friends and fans and takes orders. It's quite a profitable business.

Expert Testimony/Consulting. Do you have a special knowledge in an area that a business could benefit from by picking your brain? If so, seriously consider signing up with a company that can find you work as an expert authority. This can mean anything from providing expert testimony in a court of law or answering questions about your field of expertise over the telephone to a company. While the work will be sporadic, the hourly wage is often incredible—from about $150 per hour on up.

I really like the Gerson Lehrman Group for telephone-based consulting work (*www.glgroup.com*) and the TASA Group at for expert testimony (*www.tasanet.com*). Both are free to join, but you do need professional references and to be an authority in your field.

Newspaper Route. No, I'm not joking. If you need some additional money and don't mind getting up before the sun, than maybe delivering papers can work for you. No skills or training is required. You may even be able to take your baby with you for the ride. It can be a relatively easy way to earn some extra cash (which almost all of us can use).

Focus Groups. Again, this type of work can be sporadic and hard to find, but it can provide you with some nice spending money. Research online companies in your area that set up marketing focus groups—you can get paid to give your opinion on a variety of products and services. You usually don't need to be an expert, just a person with an opinion. The pay is typically around $50 per hour.

Home Organizing. Do you have a knack for restoring order to chaos? Do your family and friends often comment on your stellar organizational skills? If so, then consider starting your own home-organizing business. With baby in tow, you get paid to help others streamline their households and get their clutter under control. Set your own hours and have fun being your own boss. You may be surprised at how many people would pay for such a valuable service, and if you're good, word of mouth spreads fast!

Use caution when considering any "work from home" arrangements you see advertised. Some are scams. Some listing services (such as those for experts) charge an annual fee, which can be worth the investment. However, rarely is a pay-to-play job recommended. Contact the Better Business Bureau to check out complaints against the company. If you can't find information about them because they are too new, proceed with caution. Some scams reopen under different names, so remain cautious.

- The Council of Better Business Bureaus
  4200 Wilson Blvd, Suite 800
  Arlington, VA 22203-1838
  (703) 276-0100
  www.bbb.org

Deciding to work or stay at home is a very personal decision. It is one that only you and your partner (if you have one) can make. Stay true to yourself and don't let anyone pressure you into a choice that is not right for you. There is nothing worse than an unhappy, resentful, and stressed-out parent or employee. If being an SAHP is going to give you the most joy and satisfaction, do everything in your power to make it work financially. Get creative. If working outside the house is more your style and you can find a happy balance, do so with your head held high. Try not to concern yourself about social conventions and other pressures. All in all, whichever decision you make, be sure to keep the following axiom in mind: the financial security of your family is paramount.

CHAPTER SUMMARY

- Be open to all possibilities and arrangements, be true to yourself, and be realistic with your finances.
- Calculate what losing an income would mean to your overall finances.
- Understand which expenses will increase and which will decrease by one of you staying at home.
- Test eliminating an income for a few months, if you can.
- Know that you may be able to make stay-at-home parenting work by making budgetary changes.
- Consider all the ways to earn an income and remember that the choice is yours either to remain with your current employer or go out on your own.

Chapter 10

All About Child Care

Types, Facts, and Costs

UNLESS YOUR CHILD WILL be permanently attached to your hip for the next several years, chances are you'll be hiring someone to look after your baby at some point. Child care expenses can range from minimal to astronomical, and depend on a wide variety of factors, including what you need, want, and are willing to pay.

Choosing the person or agency to look after your little one shouldn't be a quick decision. If you are like the vast majority of new parents seeking child care, you're going to have to balance emotional desires with economic reality. It is a highly personal and emotional decision. There are many, often complicated, choices to make about with whom or where you leave your baby. Unless you already know and trust the person or place, leaving your child with someone can be difficult.

A word of warning: throughout your search, whether you are looking for an occasional "date night" babysitter or a full-time nanny, you may very well hear this phrase more than a few times: "You get what you pay for." It's true—*sometimes*. In many cases, the best of the best do command top dollar, but value doesn't always fit in such a neat little package. Although it would be nice to know that if you paid a tremendous amount of money, you could absolutely guarantee that your little one would have the finest care imaginable, it just doesn't always work that way. As with any occupation, some who earn top dollar salaries are worth every penny, while others aren't.

This doesn't mean that quality care doesn't exist for the money you are willing or able to pay. Oftentimes it does; you just have to make an effort to find someone who's well qualified and meets your family's needs. Some new parents have an extremely precise idea about what they want. However, rather than be rigid with your expectations, try to be open at least in the beginning. Know exactly what your options are and weigh the benefits and drawbacks of each. Try to remain flexible during this process. Sometimes, a parent's first choice doesn't match their resources or needs, which can be frustrating, but with a little time and effort, you can usually find an acceptable situation. As always, don't procrastinate: if you'll be going back to work soon after your baby is born, the caregiver question is going to come up fast, so get started with your search as early as possible.

TYPES OF CHILD CARE: AN OVERVIEW

There are several types of care arrangements that you can have for your baby, each with its own set of benefits, drawbacks, and costs. Most parents can find a comfortable situation that fits within your budget. Before making a decision on any particular option, know more about each.

Family Day Care

In almost every neighborhood in America, you'll find family day care. As the name suggests, the care is provided at an individual's home. The person who runs it may also have her own children to look after. At any given time, there can be as few as one child being cared for or several, depending on what the state allows (or even more if it is operating under the legal radar, so do careful research). The ages of children being cared for can vary, from newborns on up.

The day care operator will often provide food for your baby, which would then be embedded in the monthly fee, but parents are usually responsible for such necessities as diapers and wipes. If you feed your baby formula, you're almost always expected to provide that as well. When researching a prospective day care arrangement, make sure you have a clear picture of what is provided for your child, how much everything costs, and what you will be responsible for.

Advantages. Because there are so many of these operations in existence (currently around 300,000 regulated family day cares in the United States and countless unregulated ones), finding one that suits your needs may not be too much of a challenge. One of the most attractive aspects of family day care is that it often has the warm, cozy atmosphere that may mirror your own home. Because they are often run by a parent, perhaps even a neighbor with whom you have an established relationship, you can feel somewhat assured that the caregiver not only knows her way around a diaper but will be personally attuned to the needs of your baby.

In addition, when a neighborhood family is taking care of your child, there is a certain "it takes a village" ambiance to the care. They know you, you know them, and soon you'll know the rest of the families. This familiarity breeds a sense of responsibility, and if the care isn't up to snuff, word will get around. Parents talk.

One of the major concerns most new mothers and fathers have when leaving a newborn in someone else's care is that the baby will not receive enough loving human interaction. Every parent wants her baby to be picked up, rocked, and soothed throughout the day; the thought of your precious baby lying in a crib, crying for attention, is just too much to bear. Because many family day care businesses are, on average, fairly small, and are most often run by an experienced mother, this anxiety may be relieved. Another advantage is the opportunity for your baby to be around other children. This isn't private care; your baby will often have a rotating crew of surrogate "sisters and brothers" of varying ages to socialize with, which can be good preparation for the world around him.

Most states require home day care operators to go through a background check as well as meet specific health and safety requirements. Some family day cares are even accredited by independent agencies, often a rigorous and time-consuming process.

Disadvantages. Family day care is only as wonderful as the person running it. Therefore, even if the facility is licensed and accredited, and the worker and her staff are CPR certified, there is still no guarantee of quality care. Be aware that licensing requirements in some states are less rigid for home day cares than for child care centers. Many family day care providers have little or no background in early childhood education and development, and if you're looking for that, you may have to pay extra. In addition, if you're a working parent and absolutely need the place you leave your child to be open and available on certain days, family day care may not be the best option. Because it's often run by a single person, if he gets sick or has a family emergency, then you may have to step in and find coverage.

Some parents do not feel comfortable with the mere fact that the care is at a person's home—other neighbors and friends may come in, as well as the operator's older children and their friends. In other words, it may be *too* casual for your taste.

There are some things that you just won't see or know about family day care. If you don't want your child to be "babysat" by a television, for example, be aware that you won't know for sure that it will not get switched on once you leave, or that the caregiver won't spend a lot of time on the phone or the Internet. This is all built on trust, so trust your instincts.

Cost. Many family day cares will charge more for newborns than for older babies and children, while siblings are often discounted. Of course, the average cost varies tremendously, but by far the biggest factor in the price is where you live. It is not unheard of for full-time family day care in cities such as San Francisco, New York, and Chicago to cost around $60 per day, which translates to $1,200 per month, or $14,000 per year. In less pricey neighborhoods, the average cost drops to around $700 per month and, in some areas, can be as low as $500 per month or less. For more information about family day care, contact

- The National Association for Family Child Care (NAFCC)
  The NAFCC is a nonprofit organization that advocates
  for the family child care profession.
  5202 Pinemont Drive
  Salt Lake City, UT 84123
  800-359-3817
  www.nafcc.org

- Child Care Aware
  Child Care Aware is a program of the National
  Association of Child Care Resource and Referral
  Agencies, and it offers a child care connector hotline.
  NACCRRA
  3101 Wilson Boulevard, Suite 350
  Arlington, VA 22201
  (703) 341-4100
  www.childcareaware.org
  Child care connector hotline: 800-424-2246

- National Child Care Association (NCCA)
  NCCA is a professional trade association focused
  exclusively on the needs of licensed, private childhood
  care and education programs
  NCAA
  2025 M Street NW, Suite 800
  Washington, DC 20036-3309
  (202) 367-1133
  www.nccanet.org

Day Care Centers

A day care center is a formal child care business set up in a nonhome
environment. Some are located in churches and other religious facilities
(and may or may not be affiliated with the religion), while others are
designed to look a lot like a small school. The atmosphere at day care
centers varies widely, of course. Some have a homelike feeling, and others are more institutional in nature. As with family day care, there can be
a varying range of ages, though they often separate the older children

from the younger ones. Some are very large, with dozens of children or more, and others are very small.

Advantages. One huge advantage of a day care center is that it's usually reliable. If a caretaker is out sick, the center will find a replacement. Moreover, to operate, it must be regulated and licensed. Some accept babies as young as six weeks old, and many allow children to stay until they enter kindergarten. You don't have to negotiate pay as you often would with a nanny, a day care center won't unexpectedly quit on you, and care is available when you need it. In addition, as opposed to a family day care situation, you can usually be sure that your child will be interacting with children of the same age instead of with a lot of older or younger children. Another advantage is that the care is often well supervised and structured: they may even give you a schedule of what happens during the day (e.g., breakfast from 9:00–9:45, song time at 10:00, and so on).

If a day care center sounds good to you, just look for a place where the teacher-to-child ratios are low and groups aren't too large. Having someone interact with your child one-on-one is usually what you will be looking for, not the most toys.

Disadvantages. The last thing any parent wants is for their child to get lost among a large group of kids or be cared for by someone who doesn't have any emotional investment in the job. Because there really isn't a lot of money in it, day care workers are often young and work for minimum wage or just above. Some parents have the perception that such low-paid employees may not have the same skill set or level of interest in their job, which by no means is always true.

Cost. Pinning down a price for day care centers can be tough. Some companies have arrangements with a nearby day care center and subsidize the cost for workers. If you are low income, you may be eligible for a price break—some offer sliding scale prices. On average, day care centers are often about the same cost as family day care. Of course, the more elaborate and fancy the place, the more expensive it will be. Expect to pay somewhere between $30 and $70 per eight-hour day.

For more information about child care centers, contact

- The National Association of Child Care Professionals
  (NACCP)—a membership organization of child care
  professionals
  P.O. Box 90723
  Austin, TX 78735
  800-537-1118
  www.naccp.org

Nannies

Many parents complain about the cost of nannies. I've often heard parents say, "How does she expect me to pay that much? She'd be earning as much as I do!" Well, if that's the case for you, then a private nanny is probably not the right choice. There are other, more economical child care options out there, and just because it may seem as though everyone else has a nanny, that doesn't mean they are a necessary expense. Choose the option that best fits your resources and needs, rather than focusing on what you can't afford.

Something to keep in mind about nannies is that the definition of what one is can vary wildly. There is no strictly regulated set of qualifications that individuals must possess to consider themselves a nanny. There is quite a bit of title inflation out there; some "nannies" are actually babysitters. There are some guidelines as to what a nanny is and does, and to loosen them too much is to denigrate a hard-earned profession.

That said, there are many types of nannies out there, and some are far more affordable than others. As with everything, experience, training, references, age, languages spoken, skills that are brought to the job, and many other factors need to be considered. The cost of a nanny also depends on whether she lives in your home our outside of it, has her own child or children that she is caring for simultaneously, or if it will be a share-care situation.

Live-Out Nanny. The cost to have a private nanny who comes to you every day can vary wildly, but it's certainly not strange for a nanny to charge somewhere between $15 and $20 per hour (and more, if there are several children and the duties are complicated). Therefore, a mid-range figure would be around $18 per hour for one child. If you need child care for nine hours a day, five days a week, you are looking at $162 per day, a monthly expense of $3,240, or an annual cost of $38,880. You may also need to pay your employee's health insurance on top of that, which can be another couple of hundred dollars a month, as well as sick pay and vacation (a week or two is standard for the first year). You may be beginning to see why the expense of having a nanny is not for everyone. However, if you can handle the cost, it's a worthwhile option to consider. Having a dedicated child care professional that you've selected to meet your family's specific needs and schedule can be a wonderful resource to have at your disposal.

Live-In Nanny. If you have space in your home that you can offer to a nanny while he cares for your child and can handle the expense, you may want to consider this option. For some families, a nanny who lives in the home makes the most sense. This arrangement can really foster a close relationship between a nanny and your family.

To get a good idea of what a private live-in nanny will run, first fig-ure out the fair market rate of their living quarters. How much would someone from the outside reasonably pay for the place? Whatever that price would be, deduct it from the cost of a live-out nanny. For example, if you could rent out that extra room for $450 per month and the aver-age live-out nanny in your area charges $3,240, the approximate cost to you drops to $2,790. If food and other amenities are included, they are deducted as well.

A Nanny With Her Own Child. Some nannies are parents themselves, and seek a position where they can bring their own child to the job. This can be a terrific arrangement. The care isn't totally private, but you don't have to find another family to share the nanny with, (if you're looking to split costs) which can be very nice. Nevertheless, how much of a discount can you expect? This depends on what you negotiate with the nanny and the average cost of such an arrangement in your area. Although the ben-efit to this arrangement is that your little one has a playmate, a potential drawback may be that the biological child gets more attention.

A GOVERNESS COMEBACK

In this age of luxury and extravagance, there are those who are hell-bent on having the very best of everything. That's why governesses have been making a quiet comeback in recent years. No mere nanny, a governess is also a private teacher, educating your child in everything from ABCs to etiquette and often much, much more. Here are just a few of the responsibilities your governess may perform:

- Teacher (academic and manners) and homework assistance
- Event, party, and vacation planner (for you and the children)
- Field trip, play date, school schedule, extracurricular activity organizer
- Chauffeur
- Housekeeper
- Errand runner and private shopper for children's clothing, school supplies, and party gifts
- Menu planner
- Closet, toy, book, video, and backpack organizer
- Bathing and dressing assistant

Bottom-rung annual salaries begin at $75,000 and go beyond—way beyond—that. Obviously this isn't a realistic option for everyone, but if this fits in your budget and you want an all-inclusive child care experience for your little one, then this might be the choice for you.

Nanny Share-Care. Nanny share-care is where you get together with another family and, as the name suggests, pool the resources and expenses of a nanny. The families involved usually determine in whose home the child care will be.

Although the cost of a private nanny may be beyond the means of your family, when you share the expenses, then it becomes be a more realistic option. For example, if a private nanny charges $3,240 per month to care for a single child, and you're considering an arrangement with two children, each from a different family, the average cost per family would likely be around $1,800. The nanny benefits if each family is paying that amount because her monthly pay jumps to $3,600 per month, a substantial increase, and a well-compensated caregiver is more likely to be a happy caregiver, which is of course a very desirable quality in the person who is watching your child.

For more information about nannies and how to find the right person for you, contact

- The International Nanny Association
  2020 Southwest Freeway, Suite 208
  Houston, TX 77098
  888-878-1477
  www.nanny.org

- National Association for Nanny Care
  P.O. Box 34783
  Bethesda, MD 20827
  (202) 318-9156
  www.nannycredential.org

Mother's Helpers

Despite the gender-specific name, a mother's helper is typically a person who assists whoever the stay-at-home caregiver is with the baby and household-related chores. Often, this is a rather young person, usually a college student or teenager. Mother's helpers come in when you need them to handle various aspects of child care and may possibly run errands and do a little light cleaning, depending on the arrangement you establish. A mother's helper position may be hired on an as-needed basis, or it may be a salaried position. Essentially, the arrangement is what you make of it.

Advantages. Hiring a mother's helper is usually a very economical choice. You get the assistance you need, often from a young, energetic person who won't charge you as much as an experienced child care professional might. This is often a person who is building a resume to do more "advanced' and challenging forms of child care; perhaps he's looking to enter the nanny profession and needs to build references.

In addition, if you work from home and want the advantage of having your child cared for while you're present, a mother's helper can work well for you.

Disadvantages. If you're expecting someone who has a lot of experience with children or has special training, a mother's helper may not be your best choice. No qualifications are usually required for this type of job other than an overall enthusiasm and a desire to help. This is generally a position of very light responsibilities, reflected in the salary.

Because mother's helpers are informal caregivers, there is no government regulatory body, and finding one who fits your needs means doing your own research. I've recommended Craigslist (*www.craigslost.org*) before in this book, and I'll do it again now. In its child care section, you can search other people's postings for positions as well as post your own—all for free. A warning: Always ask for references, and make sure they are legitimate. You can even go so far as to pay for a background check.

Cost. In general, mother's helpers charge somewhere around minimum wage and slightly above. However, if your needs are above and beyond the typical duties of a "helper," the price may edge up to that of a nanny. If you'll need to leave your child alone with a mother's helper for extended periods of time, or expect her to clean and even do a little light cooking, be prepared. Again, never expect your caregiver to do more without compensating for the work appropriately.

Au Pairs

Yet another option in the spectrum of caregivers is an au pair. Au pairs are often young women, but they can also be men, typically between 18 and 26, who come from another country to live as an extended member of their host family. This is a contractual agreement that you make through an agency; the au pair provides you with up to 45 hours per week of child care in exchange for room, board, and a weekly stipend. Some of the money must go toward the au pair's educational expenses at an accredited institution. The au pair is not there to do the cooking or cleaning but to share a real cultural exchange while looking after your child.

Advantages. Besides the relatively low cost, having someone from another culture take care of your child can be a great experience for your entire family. The au pair can teach your baby a foreign language, too, and because she lives with you, there are no transportation issues to deal with. The cost to the host family is far lower than for a private nanny for many of the same features.

Disadvantages. If you are looking for something long-term, an au pair isn't it. Typically, the contract lasts for one year, maybe two. During that time, your baby can get pretty attached. He does have to live with you, too, and that sort of closeness isn't for every family—not to mention that for an au pair even to be an option, you're going to have to have the space in your home, which not every family has.

Cost. For what you get, the cost of an au pair is usually pretty remarkable. Payment is calculated based on the U.S. federal minimum wage, less an allowance for room and board. As of this writing, the average rate for au pairs is about $280 per week. Au pairs with advanced degrees will likely command a bit more, but overall, the cost is quite low. As a host family/employer you may also be responsible for a few other fees, such as an application and processing fee, which are usually nonrefundable.

A number of organizations can connect you to an au pair.

- Au Pair in America
  River Plaza
  9 West Braud Street
  Stamford, CT 06902
  800-928-7247
  www.aifs.com

- Au Pair USA
  161 Sixth Avenue
  New York, NY 10013
  (212) 924-0446
  www.aupairusa.org

Babysitters

Do you remember the days when a neighbor would call your home because they knew there was a teenage girl living there, someone who would come over at a moment's notice to baby sit for some extra cash? You may not have ever met this family or were even familiar with their children, but you would go. The parents would give a brief overview of bedtimes and dinner requirements and be off with a "We'll be back before midnight. Help yourself to snacks!"

Well, in many communities, times have changed radically, but while expectations have changed, the actual definition and job duties of a babysitter have generally remained consistent. A babysitter is there to make sure your child is safe and engaged while you're gone.

Advantages. Babysitters are usually quite flexible. A sitter may be someone you can call at a moment's notice to come by or someone you have come over on a set, regular basis.

Disadvantages. In general, there aren't any specific disadvantages to a babysitter, unless there is confusion as to what he is expected to do. In most cases, a babysitter is not hired to clean, educate your child, teach a foreign language, or provide therapeutic care. These services usually entail hiring someone more experienced and expensive.

In addition, if your babysitter is young, you may be uncomfortable about her lack of experience. If you don't know your babysitter well (perhaps this person was just referred to you by another parent), then you may be concerned about his background. In both of these cases, you have to use your own judgment, which is why it's always a good idea to do as much research as possible before making a decision. You may want your babysitter to be CPR trained and have references you can check.

Cost. Many babysitters today are similar to nannies and command (or at least demand) a comparable hourly wage. The amount you'll likely pay depends on a lot of factors, such as the going rate in your community and the age and experience of the sitter. For a rough estimate, consider what nannies are charging in your area. Babysitters are usually a dollar or two less, so if a nanny goes for $13 per hour, a babysitter may be more in the $9–$11 range. Some parents and sitters negotiate over "sleep time" rates. To you, it may seem reasonable to pay less during evening hours when the sitter isn't actively "taking care" of the baby, but the sitter may charge the same rate. There are no hard and fast rules for any of this, except that the agreement reached, as always, must work happily for all parties.

"Free" Care

If you have the option of leaving your baby with a parent, grandparent, sibling, cousin, or friend, this can be a nice way to cut down on child care expenses.

Advantages. You know and trust your family and friends. Leaving your baby with a stranger, no matter her credentials, can be scary. Moreover, all that money you save can go toward other goals, like your retirement, saving for a home purchase, or your child's higher education. In addition, there's the wonderful feeling you'll get from knowing that your child is forming a bond with someone you already love and who loves you and your baby. Many times, the friend or family member lives close by or is even willing to come to you, which can be a very convenient arrangement.

Disadvantages. Know this: As with lunches, there is no such thing as *completely* free child care. You may not have to pay with actual dollars but instead with a sense of obligation. While you won't offer up a traditional paycheck, it's a lot harder to dictate what exactly you want the child care experience to be like. In other words, it is more probable that a person or agency you hire will respect your wishes and requirements than a family member who may have their own ideas about what's best for your child and feel less inhibited about acting on them.

If you aren't paying, you lose at least some of your right to have things go exactly your way. Your parent or sibling will never be your employee. Taking care of a baby is hard work, and because they are doing it for free, you're probably going to have to allow for some differences of opinion, which can lead to resentment and relationship damage. Not only may you disapprove of certain actions, your relative may be equally as disapproving and judgmental of yours.

Cost. Well, free, sort of. If you go this route, make sure you're perfectly clear about your expectations and that the other person agrees to them willingly and happily. Yes, you'll have differences of opinion. No, the babysitter may not always follow your detailed instructions. It is simply unreasonable to expect that someone other than you will be exactly like you. Accept this possibility or go with another option. Remember to thank her for all of her efforts. Because you aren't paying in cash, your sincere appreciation or some small token can be nice compensation.

A Word About Child Care Wages:
Be the Boss You Would Want to Have

Never expect the person who works for you to do more than you have both agreed upon and are paying for. One of the most common complaints among caregivers is that parents add on chores without compensating for them or even discussing whether or not these new duties are acceptable. Other grievances are that parents don't pay on time and grumble about vacation pay or time off.

The bottom line is that regardless of how close or friendly you are with your caregiver, you are that person's employer *before* you are friends. Your relationship with your caregiver is serious business and should be both professional and respectful, including paying wages as agreed upon and on a timely basis.

The Nanny Tax. Legally, if you pay more than $1,500 (2007 figure) per year for your nanny, babysitter, or whoever takes care of your baby,* then you are responsible for paying "the nanny tax." This is actually a combination of taxes: Social Security and Medicare (called the FICA tax), federal unemployment (FUTA), and, depending on your state, state unemployment and disability taxes.

As far as FICA is concerned, both you and the nanny will owe 7.65 percent of the wages for a combined tax of 15.3 percent. How you deal with this is your choice: you may withhold the nanny's half from his paychecks or just pay a cash wage without any withholding. However, if you do the latter, you'll be required to pay the entire 15.3 percent.

* As long as it is not your spouse, parent, other child under 21, or someone under 18 whose primary job is not household employment

FUTA is due on the first $7,000 of your nanny's wages for the year, but only if you paid more than $1,000 in any calendar quarter for the current year or preceding year. The tax itself is small, only 0.8 percent, but is something to consider when factoring child care costs into your budget.

After thinking about all the taxes involved in hiring a child care expert, paying someone under the table may seem like an attractive option. However, the truth is that paying these taxes *saves* you money. If you have a dependent care FSA, you can use up to $5,000 in pretax earnings to pay for a nanny, or if that employee benefit is not available to you or you choose not to use it, you can claim the Tax Credit for Child or Dependant Care on your income tax return, which can total several thousand dollars. The nanny comes out ahead, too, because she'll likely be eligible to receive Social Security benefits and can collect unemployment. He may also qualify for the Earned Income Credit, which will put more money in his pocket at the end of the tax year.

Figuring out the nanny tax isn't easy. It's time consuming, and you will want to do it right because mistakes can be costly. This is one of those situations where I recommend hiring an outside service to help. There are quite a few companies that do this. Here are a couple that I recommend, but prices vary so do some research before deciding:

- NannyTax, Inc.
  51 East 42nd Street, Suite 601
  New York, NY 10017
  888-NANNYTAX (626-6982)
  www.nannytax.com

- Home/Work Solutions, Inc.
  2 Pidgeon Hill Drive #550
  Sterling, VA 20165
  800-626-4829
  www.4nannytaxes.com

Of course, you can do all this yourself. Check out the IRS's website for forms and information, specifically IRS Publication 926, "Household Employer's Tax Guide": *www.irs.gov.*

You should now have a good sense of the various child care options that are out there. Some may be very appealing, and others may warrant a "no way" response. On top of this, the hiring process can be laborous: finding a person or place that is right for you, your child, and your budget can take a while. Furthermore, nannies, babysitters, day care centers, and all the rest can be dreadfully expensive, so remember your future plans and balance today's needs with tomorrow's goals. In the end, make the choice that best fits your family's needs and financial circumstances.

CHAPTER SUMMARY

- Know all of your child care options and their costs.
  Options include the following:
  o Family day care
  o Day care centers
  o Nannies
  o Mother's helpers
  o Au pairs
  o Babysitters
  o "Free" care
- Before making a decision, carefully consider the benefits and drawbacks of each option, and think about which best fits into your budget.
- Be careful. The person you are hiring will be responsible for the safety and well-being of your child, so choose someone you trust.
- Be a great, fair boss: pay your child care professional on a fair and timely basis and understand how the nanny tax works.

Chapter 11

Making It Happen

Planning for Your Family's Future

PLANNING YOUR FAMILY'S FINANCIAL future can, and should, be a wonderful experience. This is the time for you to think about all of your hopes and dreams for what you'd like your lives to look like down the road. Maybe you want a spacious home with a sunny garden, an annual vacation around the globe, or a savings account with enough money in it for your child to go to Harvard without having to take out a dime in student loans. Undoubtedly, part of your goals is to ensure that your family is safe and protected from any unexpected financial pitfalls. These dreams are yours to make, and starting to think about and plan for them now is an excellent idea.

In general, planning for your family's financial future requires two key components: the first is setting a safe and secure foundation, and the second is working towards achieving your hopes and dreams. Now is the time to consider all the many things you may want to do with your money and figure out how you can achieve them.

PLAN YOUR FINANCIAL FOUNDATION

Making sure that one's family is financially stable is a universal goal. Thus, planning for your family's future means making sure that you're protected against any unexpected occurrences. An incredible number of American families live paycheck to paycheck with no monetary cushion to protect them from an unforeseen setback. Therefore, adding insurance and savings into your budget is a key part of securing your family's future and happiness. Remember that you, not your credit cards, are responsible for making sure that you are prepared for financial emergencies.

Life Insurance

If ever there was a time to purchase life insurance, the birth of your child is it. The main purpose of life insurance is to provide income replacement for your family just in case something happens to you. No one wants to think about their own mortality, but you should think about it when there are people depending on you. If you want to do everything you can to protect your baby and make sure that she is properly cared for if you're no longer around, then having life insurance coverage is a very good idea. As you're now aware, raising a baby can be astonishingly expensive. The purpose of life insurance is to make sure that your child, and anyone else who relies on you for financial support, does not suffer financially if you die before he or she has the means to take care of himself.

There are two basic types of life insurance: *term* and *cash value*. The type that is right for you depends on what you need and the premiums you can afford to pay.

Term Insurance. Term insurance is pretty simple in concept. It is designed to protect your income needs for a specific period of time. If you die within that time frame, your beneficiaries (child, partner, etc.) receive a specific sum of money, called the death benefit. In other words, if you bought a policy with a ten-year term and death benefit of $500,000, that's the amount of money your child will receive if, for some reason, you die within that ten-year period. If you're a young, nonsmoking adult, the premiums are cheap; a $500,000 policy may only set you back $25–$30 a month.

The term can range from as little as 1 year to 30 years. Your new baby will need you to take care of her until adulthood, right? Therefore, you may want a full 18 years (or more) of "childhood" protected. Maybe you just bought a home with a 30-year mortgage and you want to make sure your partner has enough money to meet the payments if you die. Take your needs and desires into consideration when deciding on the length of the term.

Be aware that term insurance does not accumulate any cash savings. Once you stop making your premiums, or if you die after the term ends, your beneficiaries receive nothing. So why get it? For the protection you receive, the cost is very low and the death benefit high. However, the older you get, the more expensive those premiums become because according to mortality charts, you're closer to dying (not to be grim, but that's the way it's figured).

Always shop around and compare insurance products. Side-by-side comparisons are easy with any of the Web-based companies that compile insurance company information. I haven't found a tremendous difference in any of the companies that do this; here are a few that are simple to use: *www.selectquote.com*, *www.intelliquote.com*, and *www.accuquote.com*.

Cash-Value Insurance. If you're interested in a policy that does accumulate cash, you may consider a cash-value, also called permanent, insurance policy. This type of product provides a death benefit as well as a built-in savings component. When you pay your premium, the insurance company invests a portion of your payment. The investment varies depending on the type of cash-value plan you choose. As long as you pay your premiums, the insurer can't cancel the policy.

Because of these factors, cash-value policies tend to cost quite a bit more than a term policy on a monthly basis. While that term policy with the $500,000 death benefit may cost only $30 per month, a cash value policy may have a premium of a couple hundred dollars. Why is there such a difference? With the term, the insurance company is banking on never having to pay out (most of the time quite accurately), but with the cash-value policy, you are building savings so you will definitely be walking away with what you put into it.

There are many varieties of cash-value policies to choose from. *Whole-life* policies have a fixed death benefit, and the premiums remain constant. The insurance company invests the savings portion in low-risk, fixed-income securities, such as treasury bills. After a few years you may borrow against it to pay for such goals as a down payment on a home or a new car. A downside to these plans is that the premiums can be quite costly, out of range for many who aren't earning a large income.

Universal life is similar to a whole-life policy. It still has the cash accumulation feature, but the premiums vary to meet your income and expense needs. With both of these products, the insurance company takes on the investment decisions.

Variable life, on the other hand, is a cash-value policy where you, not the insurance company, make the investment decisions. Some of these policies come with fixed premiums and others with flexible premiums that vary in the same way as for universal life. Be aware though, that variable life insurance is inherently risky. Sure, your investments may perform well, but then again they may not. Remember, this is insurance, not Las Vegas.

As you begin to shop around for life insurance, know that cash-value policies often come with large commissions for the seller. Don't let anyone talk you into a policy that isn't right for you or is out of your financial reach. In addition, while cash-value policies can be a good way to save money, you're usually better off buying a term policy and then saving and investing on your own.

Determine a Death Benefit. When you are trying to come up with a figure for a sensible amount of insurance protection, the general rule of thumb is this: the death benefit should be about the same amount as the policy holder's annual salary, multiplied by the number of years until your youngest child reaches adulthood or graduates from college. Therefore, if you make $45,000 a year and your baby has just been born, you would be looking for a policy with a death benefit of $990,000 ($45,000 × 22 years = $990,000). There are other factors to consider, of course. When you speak to your insurance agent, be sure to discuss all of your financial needs, such as funeral costs, medical expenses, probate costs, estate taxes, and inflation.

Don't Rely on Your Employer's Policy. If you have life insurance through your employer, chances are it's a term policy, and your company probably pays the premium. In almost all such cases, the insurance coverage won't be enough if disaster strikes. The death benefit for most employer-provided life insurance policies is usually equal to one year's salary. While something is better than nothing, if you have the opportunity to add to the policy, go for it. An extra $20 or so a month can add hundreds of thousands of dollars to the death benefit.

Life Insurance on Your Baby. Remember that life insurance is designed for income replacement. If you aren't around, the death benefit helps your beneficiaries carry on financially. Then why get life insurance on your baby? These life insurance policies are almost always cash-value plans, and while it may sound great that the money inside the policy builds up free of income taxes, they are, in general, not a great idea. Some people choose to insure their baby if they anticipate future health problems, which can make it difficult to obtain insurance at a later date. However, in most cases, these policies are heavy with sales and marketing charges, and you'd be better off taking the money and investing it yourself.

Long-Term Disability Insurance

Protecting your income if you are disabled or too ill to work is also very important. Short-term disability insurance was covered in detail in Chapter 4, but there is another type that may be good for you right now: long-term disability (LTD). This type of insurance protects you from the types of catastrophic illness or injury that can permanently end your ability to earn a paycheck and take care of your family. If you have a short-term policy, the cash benefits you would receive from a LTD policy typically begin when the other ends. You may have LTD insurance through your employer, called group coverage, or you may purchase it on your own as individual coverage.

If you don't have LTD through your employer, do consider adding it to your budget. You may never need it, but if you do, you will be thankful you did. Although the amount of income you would receive varies, most policies pay between 50 to 60 percent of your base salary for as long as you need it.

While I do believe that getting an LTD policy is a smart idea (I've seen many times how it has benefited those who could not work because of an unexpected disability), be aware that some policies can be a bit frustrating to deal with when the time actually comes to get the benefits. This doesn't mean it's not worthwhile, just that to receive the money, you're going to have to prove that you can't do your job—or depending on the policy, *any* job. Many policies provide "own occupation" coverage for a couple of years and "any occupation" coverage after that. In addition, you may need to wait until a predetermined "elimination period" ends before you receive any cash at all.

The cost for LTD policies depends on many factors, including your occupation, health, hobbies, and age. For example, let's say you are a 40-year-old new father in a professional job earning an annual salary of around $50,000. A five-year LTD policy may very well be around $1,700 a year ($141 a month) for a policy that would pay you $2,900 per month. If you have an occupation that puts you in harm's way (construction worker, perhaps), the cost of the policy would be higher. Same goes if you are a smoker, or spend each winter on the downhill slopes. If the premiums are too high for comfort, you may be able to lower them by accepting a longer elimination period.

Resources. As always, take the time to do a bit of research before you decide on any type of insurance policy. An excellent resource is the National Association of Insurance Commissioners, an organization of insurance regulators from each state: *www.naic.org*.

When shopping around, look for a company with a strong reputation. To help you make a knowledgeable decision, see how the company rates. Several good rating agencies are

- A.M. Best Company
  (908) 439-2200
  www.ambest.com

- Standard & Poor's Insurance Rating Services
  www.standardandpoors.com

- Duff & Phelps, Inc.
  www.insure.com

- Moody's Investor Services
  (212) 553-0377
  www.moodys.com

Emergency Savings

Common wisdom among financial professionals is that everybody should be saving at least 10 percent of their net income on a regular basis to make sure they're set up in the event of a crisis. In reality, we are saving on average less than 1 percent (see Figure 11.1). Americans used to be really great savers, but as a nation we're saving far less than in the past. The reasons for this discouraging state of affairs are many, including the rising cost of living, stagnant wages, and high housing costs.

Another factor that has made saving much more difficult than in previous decades is that we've lost the momentum. Rather than save, we charge. However, the truth is that saving for a possible crisis is as important as it ever has been. Borrowing your way out of an emergency may plug the dam for a little while, but it doesn't take long before you are up to your ears in debt and have a worse problem to solve. There's no doubt about it: having cash set aside for a rainy day is key. Meet this challenge

---

NEGATIVE NEWS

As far as savings goes, Americans are really not doing terribly well. If you do have some cash tucked away, you are in the minority. The U.S. Commerce Department reported that the nation's personal savings rate for 2006 was −1 percent, the worst showing in 73 years. Overall, people are spending all of the money they have left after paying taxes, and then some, by dipping into savings or borrowing to finance their current spending—a disturbing trend, to say the least.

Figure 11.1 *Personal Savings Rate Chart*

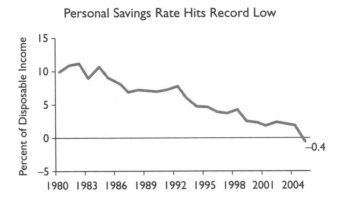

Personal Savings Rate Hits Record Low

Personal savings rate is aggregate personal saving as a percentage of disposable personal income. Aggregate personal savings are computed as total personal income after taxes minus total consumption.

Source: U.S. Bureau of Economic Analysis: 1980–2004 figures from 2006 Economic Report of the President, Table B-30; 2005 figure from the U.S. Bureau of Economic Analysis.

head-on and do whatever you can to make room in your budget for saving money on a regular basis.

How much money do you have in reserves right now? Common wisdom is that if you're caring for anyone else, then having at least a few months' worth of savings tucked away for essential expenses that you can immediately access at its full market value (i.e., not have to quickly sell an asset at a potential loss of monetary value) is crucial. Having these emergency funds can save you and your dependents from serious financial jeopardy if you lose your job or have a sudden expense.

Now that you're about to be or have just become a parent, you'll need even more in savings than what a single person needs. Rather than three months' worth set aside, think more like four to six months' worth. Sounds like a lot, doesn't it? In many cases it is, depending on your income and essential expense, but as a goal, it's an essential one. If you can achieve that, you'll have done much of what your part of being a terrific parent requires: taking care of yourself and your family, in good times and bad. Although it may be difficult, do your best to stay disciplined.

As stated, the actual dollars you need depend on your monthly expenses. To get that figure, analyze your current budget, pinpointing those expenses that are absolutely essential. These will usually be housing, food, transportation, and now, your child's expenses. Add them up to find the total, then multiply by the number of months that would cover you in a crisis. For example, if your normal monthly expenses are $3,200, but your essentials are $2,000, then a good figure for your emergency savings will be $10,000 if you want to cover yourself for five months ($2,000 × 5 = $10,000).

$10,000 may sound like a lot of money, but if you break it down into manageable monthly increments, it will be a much easier goal to achieve. For instance, if you saved it over a two-year period, it would be about $416 per month. If saving this much per month is simply not possible, don't despair; develop a realistic plan that works for you. The key is to stay disciplined and adhere to your plan.

A strategy that I have recommended to numerous clients is to set up an automatic savings arrangement with your checking account or with your employer. Simply choose the amount you want to come out of your account or paycheck each period and have it deposited into a savings account. What you don't see, you won't miss. Remember the 10 percent rule: if you make a net figure of $3,000 per month, arrange for $300 to be deducted.

Should you save money if you have debt? Yes. Begin to put aside at least a few dollars on a regular basis. Think of your child and drop change into a piggybank. Go to a bank or credit union and open a savings account. While it's true that what you set aside in a typical savings account will earn virtually no interest, and that hanging onto debt is costly, saving even a little every week or month is a powerful and positive step in the right direction. It can be horribly discouraging to pay your creditors and see nothing in the bank. Furthermore, you're developing great financial habits and establishing a pattern of positive and responsible behavior. Psychologically, saving money feels good. In addition, if you do tuck a bit away on a regular basis, by the time you repay your debt, you'll have something set aside in case of an emergency.

Emergency savings should be accessible so that if you do need to get money tomorrow, you won't be charged a penalty fee. It also needs to be nice and safe, free from wild market fluctuations and protected against personal impulses that you'll likely regret acting upon. One option is a passbook savings in a separate financial institution. Having a different savings account is a good idea because it can help protect you from the temptation of pulling from it when you run out of cash in your checking account.

A traditional savings account is FDIC insured (up to $100,000) and allows you to withdraw funds penalty-free at any time. However, remember, in exchange for total liquidity and stability, passbook savings usually provide very low investment returns.

If you want your money to earn a bit more than what it would in a typical savings account, you may also consider a money-market deposit account or a money-market mutual fund. Interest rates for money-market deposit accounts tend to be slightly higher than those of passbook savings accounts while providing a similar function. These accounts are FDIC insured, and withdrawals are penalty-free. Money-market mutual funds are not insured, but the investments mature in 13 months or fewer, so they're relatively low-risk accounts. In addition, they provide immediate access to funds without early-withdrawal penalties and typically offer higher rates of return than passbook savings and money market deposit accounts.

Don't Forget a Will

A will is nothing more than a set of instructions that specifies who gets which of your assets when you die. If you have assets, property, and loved ones, having a will drawn up should be part of your overall financial plan. If you die without one, state law takes over and makes distribution decisions on your behalf. In most cases, everything goes to your spouse and/or children. If you have neither, your closest relatives will be the recipients, and if you have no relatives, your entire estate will be absorbed by the state. While the court may make the same decisions you would have, in many cases, it does not.

One of the most compelling reasons to draw up a will is if you have children who depend on you for care. A will allows you stipulate guardianship. Without one, the court will make this very personal choice for you.

If your estate is relatively simple, you may choose to create your own will with the help of a quality software program or guidebook. For more complex situations, or if you do not feel comfortable writing your own will, hire an attorney or legal service to do it for you. The cost for a will varies, of course, but it is typically around $500 and goes up from there. Because this is such an essential document, you'll want to be sure its done right. Consider investing in a lawyer to look over your finished product at least.

PLAN FOR YOUR DREAMS

Every new parent should begin to think about what he wants the future to look like. What long-term goals do you have for the money you earn, save, and invest? Remember, your income is not just for "getting by"; it's for financing your dreams. The following section provides information on some of the most common financial goals that new parents have for their family.

Becoming a Homeowner

Is your growing family outgrowing your current living space? If so, you're not alone. Buying a new home is a common goal for new parents. Being a homeowner is a big piece of the American dream. However, even if you're seeking to buy a home in an area where ownership is relatively affordable, and you get a terrific mortgage (possibly even one that requires no down payment), you're likely going to have to come up with some cash to make that dream a reality.

The cost of buying a new home depends on a lot of factors, most notably the purchase price. You've also got the down payment to consider. If you don't have 20 percent to put down, you'll either have to purchase mortgage insurance, which will be somewhere between 0.5 percent to 0.85 percent of the loan amount until your equity reaches the full 20 percent, or get a more expensive second loan to make up the difference.

The lender will also want to know that you have some cash in reserve so that you'll still be able to continue making payments, even if something goes wrong. Having about two months' worth of payments in savings is standard, but I recommend that for your own peace of mind, you try to have a bit more than that. Of course, there are closing costs, too, which average around 3 to 5 percent of the purchase price. On average, you'll need to have about $23,000 for a $150,000 home.

Of course, there are other costs that you may need to save for. For example, you may want to buy a fixer-upper and need some immediate cash for repairs, or you may simply want to do some landscaping and redecorating or buy furnishings. Don't forget moving expenses too. Carefully factor in all housing-relating costs when estimating how much money you will need.

When determining how you'll finance the cost of buying a new home, be careful if you're considering a no-down-payment or 100-percent-financing loan. Although this might seem like an attractive option on paper, potential problems are associated with these types of loans, which can adversely affect your family's financial security. Because they provide no equity, you could end up owing more than your home is worth with even the slightest downturn in property values. There is very little, if any, margin for error if either the economy takes a hit or your own finances become shaky.

Working towards becoming a homeowner often makes a lot of sense for new parents. On top of the added space, a major benefit of owning your own home is that you get to build equity, which means you'll be building a greater degree of financial security. However, renting sometimes makes more sense for certain families. In some markets, the monthly outlay for rent is far less than it would be for a mortgage, and the costs involved in buying a new home may be much more than your budget can currently handle.

In addition, think about the benefits and drawbacks of where you live now. Is it family-friendly, with lots of parks and playgrounds? How are the local schools? Is your neighborhood safe? I strongly recommend that you take all of these factors into consideration when choosing to buy or rent.

Buying a Second Vehicle

Now that your family is growing, you may be considering an upgrade in your transportation. Do you need to trade in your old car for something safer, more reliable, or just plain bigger? Perhaps you now need a second vehicle. Whatever the situation, in most instances, you're going to need a plan to save money for this new expense. The average cost of a new car is around $28,000. Of course, very few people pay the entire amount outright. Most finance the bulk of it either through a financial institution or the dealership's financing company.

If you're like most people, you'll either trade in your old car for a newer model (assuming you have a car) or upgrade to a better vehicle. If you're a one-vehicle family and are looking to buy another, you'll want to save for a down payment, a couple of thousand dollars at least. If you just need a safer or bigger and more luxurious model, than you'll likely have to prepare for a higher monthly payment.

If a new car is part of your future plans, start researching what you want and how much it will cost so you can develop a sound financial strategy for making this major purchase. Make sure you factor in all of your family's needs and resources when determining which vehicle is right for you. A great place to begin your search is Edmunds, Inc. It has an excellent and comprehensive car buying guide online: *www.edmunds.com.*

Saving for Education

If you are thinking about paying for your child's education, get ready to set aside some serious cash. Preparing for these expenses now is a great idea.

Preschool. Preschool is different from day care; it's actual education for your child that typically begins at around two years old. That is not so far away, and time will pass quickly. So what does preschool cost? Depending on the number of days, the area you live in, and the type of preschool your child attends, the cost can be minimal or huge. A three-day, four-hour preschool experience for your child may start at around $150 per month and can go up dramatically from there. If you are looking at a full-day schedule (Monday through Friday, from around 8:00 to 5:30), the cost will often begin at $600. In expensive metropolitan neighborhoods, that price can easily shoot up to $1,500 a month.

If the cost of preschool sounds a little daunting, the Head Start program may be an option for you. This national program provides grants to local public and private agencies to provide comprehensive child development services to economically disadvantaged children and families. The primary focus is helping preschoolers develop the early reading and math skills they need to be successful in school, and the cost to you as a parent may be minimal. It is administered by the U.S. Department of Health and Human Services, and you can find a Head Start Program near you via the website: *www.acf.hhs.gov.*

Private School. If you want to look a bit farther ahead, and are thinking about sending your child to a private elementary school (and middle and high school, too, perhaps) begin thinking of that cost. Many private schools start at $12,000 per year and go up from there. If you choose a parochial school, the tuition will be a few hundred dollars to $1,000 per month and up. Of course, there is home schooling as well, and though there are costs involved for that option, they are significantly less than those for private schools.

College. Now let's look way into the future—around 18 years from now. Saving for college is a massive endeavor. If you want to pay for at least part of your child's higher education costs, there are a number of tax-advantaged ways to do so. Before you get started, though, keep in mind that almost every financial professional stresses the importance of making sure your own retirement goals are funded before you begin to set aside cash for your child's education.

At this point, you may be asking yourself, "How much will sending my child to college *really* cost me?" Well, that depends on many factors, including whether you want to pay for every penny of the entire four years or look into student loans, grants, scholarships, and other financing options as well as if your child will be going to a community college or to a private or public university, and so on.

Here are two scenarios to help give you a good idea of what the cost of higher education for your child might look like. Perhaps you want to pay all of the associated costs for your infant daughter's private college expenses. Currently, you don't have a penny saved but are raring to go. The total four-year cost of a private school 18 years from now is projected to be roughly $215,000. To reach that sum, you're going to need to set aside approximately $374 per month, starting today, assuming a conservative 7 percent return on your investment.

THE COST OF COLLEGE

Four-year public colleges
- Tuition and fee charges at four-year public colleges average $5,836.
- The average total tuition, fee, room, and board charges for in-state students at public institutions are $12,796.
- After grant aid and tax benefits are considered, full-time students enrolled in public four-year colleges and universities pay on average about $2,700 in net tuition and fees.

Four-year private colleges
- Tuition and fee charges at four-year private colleges average $22,218.
- The average total tuition, fee, room, and board charges at private four-year colleges and universities are $30,367.
- Full-time students enrolled in private colleges and universities pay on average about $13,200 in net tuition and fees after grant aid and tax benefits.

Two-year public colleges
- Tuition and fee charges at two-year public colleges average $2,272.
- After grants and tax benefits are considered, full-time students enrolled in public two-year colleges and universities pay less than $100 on average in net tuition and fees.

—*Source: 2006–07 College Board data*

On the other hand, perhaps your son will be going to a public university. If so, the cost will be substantially less, but by no means cheap. Assuming you want to pay for all related costs, the grand total will be somewhere around $100,000. On a monthly basis, you'd need to set aside about $200, starting now.

A good way to estimate the amount of what college might cost is with an online calculator. Among the best that I've found for ease of use and accuracy is the Motley Fool's online calculator at *www.fool.com/college/college01.htm.*

Although there are several ways to save for your child's education, I recommend considering the following vehicles to help you reach your goal.

Coverdell Education Savings Accounts are tax-deferred college savings accounts and can be an excellent way to save for the cost of college. Although contributions are not tax deductible, they do grow tax-free. You may open these plans at any financial institution that handles traditional IRAs, and you can use just about any investment option that works for you to build your savings. When the funds are withdrawn to pay for college expenses, the earnings are tax-free. There are restrictions, of course—the money must be used before the child reaches 30, and allowable contributions are limited for those making high incomes and are phased out entirely for very high earners. Contributions can be made by individuals with a modified adjusted gross income of less than $110,000; for a couple filing a joint return, that amount is $220,000. If there is an unused portion, or if your child doesn't end up going to college, there will be a tax consequence and a 10 percent penalty, although you can avoid this by rolling the balance into another Coverdell plan for a different family member.

If you'd like to save for your child's future higher education expenses while also reducing your tax liability, consider opening a *529 plan*. These plans come in two basic varieties: the college savings plan and the prepaid tuition program. Both are easy to set up and offer the same tax advantages. Everyone is eligible to take advantage of a 529 plan. There are no income limitations or age restrictions.

The most popular type of 529 is the *college savings plan*. Every state in America now has at least one college savings plan available. You may use whichever state's plan you like and invest the money in any accredited college or university in the United States. Each state's college savings program offers several different investment choices, so look for the plan that best meets your financial needs. For example, some start with aggressive investments, and as the time nears for their child to go to college, they gradually become more conservative. Some have a "guaranteed option," which protects your principal (meaning the investments are very low risk) but also provides for a minimum of growth.

Prepaid tuition plans allow you to purchase all or part of the cost of a future public, in-state education at today's prices. The value of your investment is guaranteed at least to meet college tuition inflation. This can give you and your family real peace of mind. The plans offer a better rate of return than savings vehicles, your contributions are completely safe, and your investments are often guaranteed or backed by the state. You don't lose the money if your child decides to attend a different college than the one you saved for, though there may not be enough to cover the new college's cost. You (or your child) will have to come up with the difference.

With both college savings and prepaid tuition plans, as long as you use the investment for qualified education expenses, you won't have to pay income tax on the earnings. If you use your own state's plan, you may also qualify for a state tax deduction (contributions to state plans are not deductible on your federal tax return). Be careful about taking money out for something other than education purposes. If you do, the earnings portion of the "nonqualified" withdrawal will be subject to income tax, and you'll be hit with a 10 percent penalty tax. Some states even pile on another 10 percent penalty.

One of the benefits of a 529 plan is that you don't have to do much to manage the account. Either the state treasurer's office or an investment company that is hired as the program manager does that for you. All these professionals come with a price though: management and fund fees can be high, in some cases even outweighing the plan's benefits. In addition, several plans charge one-time enrollment fees, which range from $10 to $90.

To know what each state is offering and to compare and contrast plans, visit the College Savings Plans Network's website at *www.collegesavings.org* or visit *www.savingforcollege.com.* Many financial institutions offer information about 529 plans to help you decide whether or not to enroll. After you decide which 529 plan to use, you just need to complete a simple form and make your first contribution, which can be as low as $25. Be sure to sign up for automatic deposits to make savings easy.

A *custodial account* is a gift to your child wherein all assets held in the account are legally his. These accounts are generally less restrictive than other college-planning methods, with no income limitations or contribution ceilings, and withdrawals are not restricted to higher-education uses. However, custodial accounts do not come with the tax-deferred growth that some other vehicles offer, where you pay the tax upon withdrawal. While your child is a minor, you retain control over the assets. However, after your child reaches age 18, the money automatically shifts to her. Only the first several hundred dollars of the investment earnings accumulate tax-free; the rest is taxable. Also, keep in mind that distributions can hurt your child's chance of getting financial aid. Assets that are owned by the child are factored in much more heavily than those owned by the parents when determining how much financial aid he qualifies for. You can set up a custodial account at a bank or brokerage firm.

Yet another way to save for your child's higher education is with *bonds.* The Education Bond Program allows you to protect the interest you earn on Series EE savings bonds from federal income tax. These bonds are reliable, low-risk, government-backed savings tools that you can use toward financing your child's education as well as other goals. To reap the tax advantage, you must meet certain income and age guidelines, the bonds must be registered in your name, and you must pay for the higher-education expenses in the same calendar year in which you redeem the bonds. You can buy these bonds and get additional information on the U.S. Treasury's website: *www.treasurydirect.gov.*

Zero coupon bonds are another option. You buy them at a deep discount, then redeem them for their face value when they mature. For example, you may buy a ten-year, zero-coupon bond that has a face value of $10,000. If the implied yield (interest) is 6 percent, it will cost you $5,537. Ten years from now, you will receive the full $10,000. They don't have the same tax advantages of other college savings options, but they can be a smart addition to other plans. You can buy these bonds at any brokerage firm.

Planning for Fun: Vacations

With all the hard work and planning for your new baby going on, you may very well be too exhausted even to think about vacations right now. On the other hand, perhaps that's all you can think about! Although I strongly recommend that you prioritize your family's financial goals and plan carefully for all essential expenses first, planning for a pleasure, such as for a family vacation, is a wonderful way to reward yourself.

Start to think about the sort of trip that you might want to take. Maybe you have relatives or friends who live on the opposite coast or

VACATION, TAKE-OUT, OR COLLEGE?

A 2006 study by AllianceBernstein Investments found that half of parents surveyed spent more on vacations in the past year than they saved for their kids' college funds. Even more startling was the finding that 58 percent spent more on dining out or ordering take-out. Overall, parents tend to overestimate the amount of financial aid available, and the majority of those surveyed believed that their kids have special talents that would make them worthy of scholarships. They also failed to adjust the cost of college over years of inflation. Seventy percent of parents who expect their children to go to college don't have a financial plan in place to help them meet their goals.

in another country that you'd like to visit. Is there a specific locale that you've always dreamed of going to? What would it cost? Estimate the total price and then begin to save. Let's take a look at an example. If you're a family of three traveling from Chicago to San Diego, roundtrip airfare alone could easily set you back $1,500. That's just over $100 a month if you plan on taking off a year from now. If it's too expensive, think of ways that you can reduce this figure. On many airlines, infants fly for free provided you hold that precious bundle on your lap the whole time. Although this may not be particularly comfortable, especially on long flights, it might be worth it to you. Alternatively, maybe you'd rather wait a few months and save more. The choice is yours.

Wherever you want to go, calculate all related expenses, including hotel accommodations, meals, transportation, entertainment, and so on (remember to shop around and be willing to negotiate to get the best deals), and calculate a rough total for your family trip. Now, develop a plan to save the money for your trip. As with all goals, break the price down into realistic monthly installments so that it isn't too taxing on your family's budget.

Planning for Other Big-Ticket Items

Think about anything else that you may want to save for—things you really want and that will make your family's life more pleasurable. Perhaps it's a flat-screen television for all of those evenings in rather than nights out on the town? Maybe it's a houseful of beautiful new furniture?

Maybe you want to create a backyard wonderland full of state-of-the-art playground equipment or a pool for your baby's first swim? Give some real consideration to all of the fun things in life that you want. They are most definitely part of your dreams, too, and as long as you don't sacrifice more important goals to get them, you should add them to your savings plans. Money isn't just a safety net; it's for enjoyment as well. Preparing for these types of big-ticket expenses can keep you motivated to save for more vital long-term expenses.

This chapter is not meant to overwhelm you with all of the expenses that you may want or need to start thinking about and preparing for. It's designed to open your eyes to the very real costs of planning for your family's future, inspire you to take action, and provide you with advice and guidelines for doing so in a financially sound way. Having dreams for the future is wonderful, but isn't it so much better when you can make those dreams a reality?

CHAPTER SUMMARY

- Planning your family's financial future can be a wonderful and incredibly positive experience.
- Use sound financial planning to achieve all of your family's short- and long-term financial goals.
- Plan your financial foundation:
  - Use life insurance to protect your income in case you die.
  - Consider long-term disability insurance to protect your income in case you are seriously injured or ill.
  - Set up an emergency savings account to protect against a financial crisis.
  - Have a will drawn up to protect your assets and set up guardianship in case you die.
- Plan for your dreams:
  - Prioritize your family's dreams and develop a healthy financial strategy for achieving them.
  - Save for homeownership or a move to a different neighborhood.

- o Consider saving for a new, second, or better vehicle.
- o Start thinking now about setting aside money for education costs.
- o Don't forget fun—if you are going to travel, set aside money for it.
- Don't let the cost and effort of planning for all of your family's goals and dreams overwhelm you: let it motivate you to get started planning now!

Chapter 12

Road Map to Success

Creating Your Family Budget

THE TIME HAS COME for a new beginning. Creating a comprehensive family budget is a powerful plan for ensuring the security and happiness of your loved ones. Now that you have a clear picture of your income, resources, expenses, and goals, you can determine precisely what you want your family finances to look like. You're armed with key information neccesary to make positive and lasting change.

If you're hesitant to move forward, know this: a budget is quite simply the best and most effective tool to eliminate monetary waste from your life; determine what things to buy, save for, or avoid; and secure your family's immediate and long-term financial well-being, no matter what comes up in your life. Your new budget will be your road map for your family's financial future. It will enable you to see where you've been, know where you are, and chart where you are going. Creating it should be an exciting experience. This is your opportunity to realistically plan for everything you want out of life.

YOUR NEW FAMILY BUDGET

How is your income changing because of your new baby? Are you going to work part-time or full-time, change jobs (and income), or not work at all? Will you be collecting child and/or spousal support payments? Whatever the changes are, a crucial step in developing your family's budget is calculating your total monthly income. Again, be sure to include any variable income you receive each month. If your income will be temporarily reduced, be sure to note when it will go back up. It you plan on going back to work on a reduced schedule, then make a note of what your new income will be. You don't want to be caught off guard by not having enough money coming in to support yourself and your family in the manner that you desire. This is the time to consider every financial possibility, to develop the most precise and comprehensive budget possible.

Review each expense category carefully and begin to make key decisions—what stays the same, what goes, and what can be realistically reduced. You will be including all those new monthly baby expenses as well as setting aside money for each of your savings goals. Keep in mind that most people greatly underestimate the amount they spend, so make every effort to be honest and accurate.

Up-front Costs
In Chapter 1 you completed a net worth statement, listing all of your assets, including what each is and what each is worth. With a new baby here or on the way, you also have some new costs to consider, some of which can be pretty significant. Is there money in your checking or savings accounts that can pay for it all? Would you consider selling some property or other assets to cover the costs? Everything should be analyzed for its benefits and consequences.

For example, if you sell some stock to help pay for all the new baby items you'll need, you will probably have to pay taxes on the gains next year. In that case, you have to plan for that, too. Weigh every reasonable option as you move forward to develop your savings and spending strategy.

That said, some assets should be considered somewhat "untouch-able," such as any money that you've built into your retirement fund. Only under the most extreme of binds should you deduct any money from what you've saved for your later years. Any home equity, too, should be tapped only after a meticulous financial analysis. Exhaust all other alternatives first and get creative if necessary. Selling some of your unnecessary things in a garage sale or in an online auction can be a way to earn some quick cash. You'll not only get rid of some clutter but perhaps make a few hundred dollars that can pay for some of baby's new things.

As discussed, another way to pay for immediate baby costs is by charging them to your credit cards. This is fine, as long as you repay them when the bills come in or, at the most, over the next few months. Assuming that you've refined your must-have list to the key essentials, borrowing responsibly and using your credit cards as the short-term loan payment tools that they are is perfectly acceptable behavior. As an added benefit, you do get all the consumer protection plastic provides plus maybe get some cash-back rewards or rack up some airline miles, and you'll be simultaneously building a positive credit score—something you'll need for future borrowing opportunities.

So what do you need to purchase for your growing family that you haven't already? In Chapter 5, you learned what health, fertility, adoption, parent education, and so forth will run. In Chapter 6, you figured out the amount of money it's going to take to pay for all the baby items you'll need and want in the coming months. Some of these expenses will be one time costs, others will be ongoing budget items. You'll see categories for all of these expenses in the following new family budget worksheet (Figure 12.3).

New Family Goals

Now that you have a clearer sense of your family's short- and long-term financial goals, how are you going to achieve them? A little planning, and a lot of hard work and discipline, goes far.

Plan Your Goals. To organize and plan for your financial goals, look carefully at the new family goals worksheet in Figure 12.3 and follow this simple, five-step process:

1. Mark off which goals you would like to save for in the **Y/N** column. If you have a goal that's not on the list, write it in.
2. List the actual amount you need to achieve each goal in the **Total Cost** column.
3. When do you want to achieve your goal? Mark it in the **Target Date** column.
4. In the **Months/Years Until Target Date** column, break down the number of months you have until your target date.
    a. If the target date for a goal is long into the future, simply multiply the number of years by 12 to get the number of months you have to save (e.g., 17 years × 12 months in a year = 204 months).
    b. If you're going to depend on accumulated interest to help you reach your goal, I suggest using an online financial calculator to get an accurate estimate of what you'll need to save. I recommend the ones at Bankrate.com: *www.bankrate.com.*
5. How much do you need to set aside every month to get what you want? Divide the total cost by the number of months you have until your target date and add the figure to the **Savings per Month** column.

Let's look at an example. You're developing a monthly savings plan for achieving the goal of financing your child's college education, while ensuring you have enough money set aside in case of an unexpected emergency. Your worksheet might look like Figure 12.1.

Figure 12.2 illustrates the challenges Americans face with saving money. Using the new family goals worksheet to develop a solid monthly savings strategy can help you successfully begin saving.

Now it's time to complete your own new family goal worksheet. Although it's best to use exact numbers, if you have to estimate, then try

Figure 12.1 *Sample Education Goal Worksheet*

Y/N	Goal	Total Cost	Target Date	Months/ Years Until Target Date	Savings per Month
Y	Emergency Savings	$6,000	June 2010	18 months	$333
Y	College/ Education Fund	$127,520	2025	17 years/ 204 months	$268
Total Savings Goal: $333 + $268 = $601 per month					

Figure 12.2 *Where Does it Hurt?*

WHERE DOES IT HURT?		WHERE'S THE SPLURGE?	
Which of your regular and other expenses do you have the most trouble affording?		What kind of expenses do you splurge the most on?	
Home and housing	16%	Food and dining out (NET)	25%
Cars (NET)	11%	Entertainment and recreation (NET)	17%
Bills and utilities (NET)	10%		
Entertainment and recreation (NET)	6%	Shopping and personal items (NET)	15%
Medical (NET)	5%	Home and housing (NET)	7%
Children and schooling (NET)	4%	Children and schooling (NET)	7%
Food and dining out (NET)	3%	Bills and utilities (NET)	4%
Taxes (NET)	3%	Cars (NET)	3%
Shopping and personal items (NET)	2%	Medical (NET)	1%
Insurance (general mentions)	1%	Luxury items (general mentions)	*
Luxury items (general mentions)	1%	Credit card payment	*
Credit card payment	1%	Insurance (general mentions)	*
Other	5%	Taxes (NET)	*
Nothing	28%	Other	4%
Don't know	10%	Nothing	14%
		Don't know	6%

Notes: Based on half-sample of 1,008 respondents. Responses total to more than 100 percent because respondents could offer more than one answer to these open-ended questions.

Source: We Try Hard, We Fall Short. Americans Assess Their Saving Habits, Pew Research Center Study, January 24, 2007.

Figure 12.3 *New Family Goals Worksheet*

Y/N	**Goal**	**Total Cost**	**Target Date**	**Months/ Years Until Target Date**	**Savings per Month**

Y/N	Goal	Total Cost	Target Date	Months/Years Until Target Date	Savings per Month
	Home Down Payment				
	Retirement Savings				
	New/Second Car Costs				
	Emergency Account				
	Vacation Fund				
	Investment Account				
	College/Education Fund				
	Fertility/Adoption Costs				
	Big-ticket Item				
	Big-ticket Item				
	Other Savings Goal				
	Other Savings Goal				
	Other Savings Goal				

NEW FAMILY GOALS WORKSHEET

Total Savings Goal:

Notes:

to be as realistic as possible. Then, in the notes section, write a reminder that you'll need to do some research to get an exact figure so that you can determine what the goal will really cost.

When you're done completing your worksheet, total the amount of savings you'll need per month to reach all of your goals. If the number sounds impossibly high, go back and reprioritize. Is the new car more important than the new furniture? Is saving for a vacation more important than saving for a down payment on a home? Consider reducing or extending the time you allow yourself to achieve each goal to meet your needs. You'll be using these monthly figures in order to complete the upcoming cash flow worksheets, so you want to get these figures as accurate and realistic as possible.

Crunching the Numbers

To make things easier, your new budget will be constructed using the following worksheets, divided by major spending and saving categories, which allows you to focus separately on each aspect of your finances.

Figure 12.4—Income
Figure 12.5—Savings
Figure 12.6—Housing and home maintenance
Figure 12.7—Unsecured debt
Figure 12.8—Baby expenses
Figure 12.9—Food
Figure 12.10—Medical and health
Figure 12.11—Transportation
Figure 12.12—Personal clothing and accessories
Figure 12.13—Education
Figure 12.14—Personal care
Figure 12.15—Entertainment
Figure 12.16—Miscellaneous

You'll notice that each budget worksheet has Old, New, and Future columns. The Old is for what you have been spending your money on, before you make any changes. The New is for your proposed changes, from now into the next year. For example, you may have $250 listed in the Old column for dining out but decide that you will cut that down to half. The Future column is for longer-term projections. Are there any expenses that you expect to increase or decrease 12 months from now?

Under each category, there is room for notes. This is where you should jot down things such as who will take on what tasks. Will you or your partner look into insurance coverage, the date one of your credit cards is paid off, or researching child care costs. It is a place for planning

Figure 12.4 *Income Worksheet*

INCOME WORKSHEET			
Source	**Old**	**New**	**Future**
Employer 1			
Employer 2			
Retirement/Pension			
Child Support			
Spousal Support/Alimony			
Social Security			
Government Benefits			
Unemployment Insurance			
Disability Insurance			
Support From Family/Friends			
Investments (rental property, dividends, etc.)			
Other			
Other			
Total Income:			
Income Notes:			

and key information. With everything that's going on in your life right now, it can be easy to forget even important tasks, so try to keep track of your intentions as well as your research. You'll be glad that you did.

Income. Use the income worksheet (Figure 12.4) to assess your family's current total income as well as track any financial changes you may be experiencing or anticipating in the near future.

Savings. As you're now aware, setting aside money in savings is essential. In the new family goals worksheet, you figured out the necessary monthly savings for you to achieve each of your goals. Include the cost

Figure 12.5 *Savings Worksheet*

SAVINGS WORKSHEET			
Savings Purpose	**Old**	**New**	**Future**
Home Down Payment			
Retirement Savings			
New/Second Car Costs			
Emergency Account			
Vacation Fund			
Investment Account			
College/Education Fund			
Fertility/Adoption Costs			
Big-ticket Item			
Big-ticket Item			
Other Savings Goal			
Other Savings Goal			
Total Savings:			
Savings Notes:			

in your savings worksheet (Figure 12.5). You may find that adding this in will throw off your budget, which means you'll have to make some deci sions. Don't underestimate the benefit of prioritization! Cutting back on areas that aren't important to you will free up cash for things that you really need or want.

Housing and Home Maintenance Expenses. When developing a budget, it's important to have a good idea of your housing and home maintenance expenses. With your new baby, perhaps there'll be some significant changes in this area to analyze. Are you moving or planning for a move? If you are, include the new rent or mortgage on your work-sheet. Remember that larger homes require more energy to heat and cool, so make sure you estimate this change.

Figure 12.6 *Housing and Homecare Expenses Worksheet*

HOUSING AND HOMECARE EXPENSES WORKSHEET			
Expense	Old	New	Future
Rent/Mortgage			
2nd Mortgage/Equity Line			
Condo Fees/HOA Dues			
Property Taxes			
Homeowner's/Renter's Insurance			
Time Shares			
Gas/Electric			
Property/Land			
Water/Sewer/Garbage			
Cable/Satellite			
Telephone			
Cell Phone/Pager			
Maintenance/Cleaning			
Pool Service/Gardening			
Monitored Alarm			
Pet Expenses			
Banking Fees/Postage			
Household Items			
Internet Service			
Other Home Care			
Other Housing			
Total Housing Expenses:			
Housing Notes:			

A major benefit to completing this chart is to help you see the larger picture and to determine if there are any expenses in this category that you can reasonably reduce. Maybe it's time for a new cell phone plan or to give up a time share or second piece of property. Do you pay for any

Figure 12.7 *Unsecured Debt Worksheet*

UNSECURED DEBT WORKSHEET			
Debt Source	**Old**	**New**	**Future**
Credit Card			
Credit Card			
Credit Card			
Credit Card			
Credit Card			
Credit Card			
Credit Card			
Bank/Credit Union Loans			
Medical Debt			
Legal Debt			
Student Loans			
Personal Loans			
Other Debt			
Total Unsecured Debt:			
Unsecured Debt Notes:			

cleaning services? If one of you will be staying home, maybe that expense can be dropped. Perhaps you can combine your telephone service with cable and Internet for a better overall rate. Again, consider all of your options and remember what's most important to you. Making a cut in some less-than-crucial area may mean a minor inconvenience, but if it also means that you have a greater chance of achieving an important financial goal, then isn't it worth it?

Unsecured Debt. If you've got unsecured debt, plan to get rid of it! Again, this is a category that requires prioritization. Make a plan to reduce and eliminate your unsecured debt and stay committed to achieving this goal. You and your family will be glad that you did.

Figure 12.8 *Baby Expenses Worksheet*

BABY EXPENSES WORKSHEET			
Expense	Old	New	Future
Child Care: day			
Child Care: evening			
Diapers: service or disposables			
Baby Wipes			
Clothes			
Toys			
Accessories: pacifiers, blankets, etc.			
Nutrition: formula, nursing expenses, future food			
Personal Care: special soaps, lotions, diaper cream, etc.			
Other Baby Expenses			
Total Baby Expenses:			
Baby Expenses Notes:			

Baby Expenses. Your baby will either be born soon or is already here. What are the things you'll need for her on a monthly basis? As you may have already figured out, it can be astounding how much newborn and infant expenses can be, depending on what you consider essential and what you consider a luxury. For example, if you plan on lavishing your baby with many outfits, add in what you think you may honestly spend. To get you started on the right track, remember that the average parent spends around $50 per month on a new baby's wardrobe.

Food Expenses. When calculating food expenses, be as comprehensive as possible. Also, when looking at the "dining out" category, know that doesn't mean just white tablecloth meals—it also includes take-out, such

Figure 12.9 *Food Expenses Worksheet*

FOOD EXPENSES WORKSHEET			
Expense	**Old**	**New**	**Future**
Groceries			
Dining Out			
Breakfast			
Lunch			
Dinner			
At Work/School			
Other Food and Snacks			
Total Food Expenses:			
Food Notes:			

as pizza, Chinese food, and fast food, which can really add up. If either you or your partner will be a stay-at-home parent, then your lunches out and snack expenses will most likely be decreased. However, unless you really won't be going out at all, don't get rid of them entirely. Many people can reduce the amount of money they spend on groceries with foresight and bargain hunting. This may be the perfect time and area for you to get in touch with your frugal side.

Calculating food expenses can be a challenge, and you may be wondering how much other families are spending. Therefore, if you want to base your supermarket spending on national averages, here's a guide.

According to a recent USDA Center for Nutrition Policy and Promotion study, the average American family of four with two children ages five and under spent $100 a week on a thrifty food plan, $154.90 on a moderate plan, and $191.10 on a more liberal spending plan. A family of four with one child age six to eight and a second child between the ages of nine and eleven spent $115.80 on a thrifty food plan, $185.60 on a moderate plan, and $224.70 on a more liberal plan.

Figure 12.10 *Medical and Health Expenses Worksheet*

MEDICAL AND HEALTH EXPENSES WORKSHEET			
Expense	Old	New	Future
Health/Dental Insurance			
Regular Prescriptions			
Regular Doctor's Visits			
Pre/Postnatal Medical: copayments, medications, other procedures			
Baby Medical: copayments, medications			
Other Medical			
Total Medical Expenses:			
Medical and Health Notes:			

Medical and Health Expenses. With a new baby, the medical and health expenses category is one where you'll most likely see a significant increase. Are you going to be purchasing health insurance or bumping up an existing policy? Add in all increased copayments, anticipated doctor's visits, and prescription costs, doing your best to be as accurate as possible.

Transportation Expenses. Have you determined that your growing family needs a bigger vehicle? Are you planning on buying a new or used car or trading up for a safer ride? If so, include the cost of the new payment in your budget as well as the increased insurance coverage and fuel costs. If you have a trade-in, make sure this is factored into your total transportation expenses. In addition, if one of you will be a stay-at-home parent, perhaps some of the driving expenses will decrease, so consider that as well.

Personal Clothing and Accessories Expenses. Many women's bodies change after they give birth, which may mean that new clothes are

Figure 12.11 *Transportation Expenses Worksheet*

TRANSPORTATION EXPENSES WORKSHEET			
Expense	**Old**	**New**	**Future**
Vehicle Payment #1			
Vehicle Payment #2			
Gasoline			
Maintenance/Repairs			
Insurance			
Registration			
Tolls/Parking			
Public Transportation			
Other Transportation			
Total Transportation Expenses:			
Transportation Notes:			

Figure 12.12 *Personal Clothing and Accessories Expenses Worksheet*

PERSONAL CLOTHING AND ACCESSORIES EXPENSES WORKSHEET			
Expense	**Old**	**New**	**Future**
Clothing			
Jewelry			
Accessories			
Laundry/Dry Cleaning			
Other Clothing			
Total Clothing Expenses:			
Personal Clothing and Accessory Notes:			

Figure 12.13 *Personal and Parental Education Expenses Worksheet*

PERSONAL AND PARENTAL EDUCATION EXPENSES WORKSHEET			
Expense	**Old**	**New**	**Future**
Tuition			
Lessons			
Materials			
Other Education			
Total Education:			
Education Notes:			

Figure 12.14 *Personal Care Expenses Worksheet*

PERSONAL CARE WORKSHEET			
Expenses	**Old**	**New**	**Future**
Haircuts/Color			
Cosmetics			
Manicures/Pedicures			
Spa Treatments			
Other Personal Care			
Total Personal Care Expenses:			
Personal Care Notes:			

needed. Again, being a smart shopper can really help you cut costs in this category.

Personal and Parental Education Expenses. Consider your future employment goals and plans for intellectual growth. Do you need to get an advanced degree or certification to move to the next level of your job?

Figure 12.15 *Entertainment Expenses Worksheet*

ENTERTAINMENT EXPENSES WORKSHEET			
Expense	**Old**	**New**	**Future**
Movies/Video			
Dining Out			
Sports/Hobbies/Clubs			
Vacation/Travel			
CDs/Tapes/Videos/DVDs			
Books/Magazines			
Other Entertainment			
Total Entertainment Expenses:			
Entertainment Notes:			

If so, what will it cost on a monthly basis? Maybe you want to take regular parenting classes. Whatever your educational goals are, factor all related expenses here.

Personal Care Expenses. What does it cost to keep you looking and feeling great? Compile all personal care expenses here. Remember, if you're looking to cut down on nonessentials so you can cover more pressing expenses, this may be a good area to concentrate on. It's your choice; just keep your goals in mind. If you can't meet your more basic expenses, you're going to have to cut down somewhere or find a way to increase your income.

Entertainment Expenses. Many new parents find that this is the one area of their budget that is *naturally* reduced. You're simply too tired to go out and spend money! Then again, you may be adding a subscription to a few parenting magazines, or you may want to join a gym to get back in shape . . . maybe not *right* now, but perhaps a year from now. As always, keep your larger goals in mind when allocating funds for non-essentials.

Figure 12.16 *Miscellaneous Expenses Worksheet*

MISCELLANEOUS EXPENSES WORKSHEET			
Expense	**Old**	**New**	**Future**
Taxes			
Life Insurance			
Other Insurance			
Union Dues			
Ongoing Legal Fees			
Storage Fees			
Cigarettes/Alcohol			
Gifts			
Religious/Charitable Contributions			
Other Miscellaneous			
Other Miscellaneous			
Other Miscellaneous			
Total Miscellaneous Expenses:			
Miscellaneous Notes:			

Miscellaneous Expenses. Here's the spot to consider all those things that just don't fit in any of the other categories. Some of these expenses are discretionary and can be cut (do you really need that storage unit—and there couldn't be a better time than now to quit smoking!); others you might need to add.

Crunch the Numbers

After you've completed the previous worksheets, take a deep breath and add up the totals for each of the Old, New, and Future columns. Subtract these figures from your projected income. Where does that leave you? You may find that you're able to meet all of your expenses and even have some cash left over. If that's the case, congratulations, you're in good shape! Add the remaining cash to your goals or other expenses.

On the other hand, you may see that you don't have enough cash flowing in to do all of the things you want. What are you going to do about it? Remember, you control your money, not the other way around! A deficit is not acceptable, because it will only lead to debt and anxiety for you and your family. Think of ways you can make things work. Can you do any of the following:

- Increase your income—in what way and by how much?
- Decrease your expenses—what can be reduced or eliminated?
- Delay your goals—how far back are you willing to wait for one or more of your financial objectives?

Often, the best way to come out even or ahead is to adopt a combination of all of these strategies. Focus on what appeals to you most, based on your current financial situation and needs. For some people, giving up a specific lifestyle is just too painful, so they opt for taking on more hours at work or getting a part-time job to supplement their income. For others, increasing income is the least attractive or most difficult option so they look at reducing expenses.

Again, your *expenses must fit within your income.* You should have a pretty clear idea of why you want certain things. Think hard about your financial values and be aware of them as you go about reworking your family budget. Keep making positive changes until you are satisfied. Above all, be honest with yourself about what you are capable and willing to do to reach your goals and secure your family's financial well-being.

Take Action

You are likely making some very powerful decisions about your finances right now. After making these decisions, it is time to follow through and take action. If you've decided to cut your cable TV to buy some special things for your new baby, then make that phone call to the cable company right away. One by one, make these changes to ensure that you and your family are getting the most out of your money and securing your overall financial future. Don't delay or decide to put things off any longer.

Never underestimate your strength and ability to change and adjust. You know that financial security is not about acquiring more and better things. It's about taking care of yourself and your growing family by using the money that you have coming in efficiently and preparing for whatever long-term objectives that you've set, according to your own value system. The pressure to spend money can be intense right now, but you must remain strong. Shop mindfully and make sure that your essential expenses and goals are taken care of *before* you splurge. There's absolutely nothing wrong with treating yourself—*after* you've taken care of the basics.

The Bottom Line

Right now, that baby of yours is either on the scene or about to make a grand entrance. Becoming a first-time parent is one of the most exhilarating life experiences that anyone can ever have. Parenthood is full of unexpected twists and turns, but this unpredictable aspect is often part of the thrill. The last thing you want is for anything to get in the way of concentrating on being the best parent you can be while enjoying every moment of your baby's life. You don't want to be burdened by money troubles or have any kind of economic uncertainty hanging over you and your loved ones. Getting your finances in order can give you real peace of mind, something you can't buy in any store.

By now, you've learned where your finances are today, and have an idea of where you'd like them to be to make your dreams come true. You also know a bit more about your money values and how to refine them to be a positive role model for your child. If you're a single parent, you understand what you need to do to make your journey more secure; if you're part of a couple, you know the importance of communicating openly about economic issues and how to compromise for the greater good.

Protecting your family's finances can indeed be a challenge. There's so much to consider and so much at stake. However, be confident that you can plan for all the costs associated with bringing your baby home and keeping him or her happy and healthy, find child care that meets your needs and budget, and spend on what you love while preparing for the future. Financial security is one of the most precious gifts you can offer your child. It allows you the freedom to focus on parenting while providing you with an incredible sense of achievement and control. You have the reins: now lead your family into a protected and prosperous future.

Acknowledgments

THIS BOOK WOULD NOT have been possible without the love and support of the following people:

Steve Armstrong
Antoinette Banks
Liza Lyons
Lisa Sandberg

Special thanks to Roberta Sandberg, my incredible mother.
Lillian: May you grow up to be strong, secure, and independent.

Index

About the Author

ERICA SANDBERG IS A nationally recognized credit and money management authority with over a decade of experience delivering personal finance and industry information to consumers, businesses, the media, and in courts of law. During her tenure at Consumer Credit Counseling Service of San Francisco, she has helped thousands of individuals and families improve their financial standing, led countless educational workshops, and acted as agency spokesperson as the financial education and communications advisor. Ms. Sandberg is a frequent money management correspondent in the Bay Area, most notably as the credit expert for KRON-TV. On a national level, she lends her expertise to such news outlets as National Public Radio, *Money* magazine, and MarketWatch and is featured in the 2005 and 2007 PBS series *MoneyTrack*.

A published author, her personal finance articles have appeared in various magazines and trade journals, and her numerous licensed workshops are taught in credit unions nationwide. Ms. Sandberg holds a BA from San Francisco State University, a certificate in personal financial planning from the University of California—Berkeley, and a certificate in consumer credit counseling. She is a member of the Financial Planning Association of San Francisco and is an advisory committee member for Project Money. Ms. Sandberg's passion is helping people of all income levels become and remain financially independent. She and her husband live in San Francisco, California, with their daughter Lillian.